684.082

M 23-17

ID No: 97002412

Dewey No:

Date Acq:

D1685579

97002412

This book is due for return on or before the last date shown below.

11. JUL 2002

-4. OCT 2002

29. NOV 2002

20. MAY 2008

1 1 MAR 2014

Don Gresswell Ltd., London, N.21 Cat. No. 1207   DG 02242/71

Woodworking Tools
and How to Use Them

Woodworking Tools and How to Use Them

Jack Hill

Based on the classic work by
ALFRED P. MORGAN

DAVID & CHARLES
Newton Abbot   London

ID No:

Dewey No:

Date Acq:

PETERLEE TECHNICAL
684.082
M23-17
COLLEGE LIBRARY

British Library Cataloguing in Publication Data

Hill, Jack
    Woodworking tools and how to use them.
    1. Woodworking tools
    I. Title   II. Morgan Alfred P. Tools and how to
    use them for woodworking
    621.9   TT186
    ISBN 0-7153-8058-3

This book was originally published in 1948 by Crown Publishers Inc
under the title *Tools and How to Use Them for Woodworking*.
It has been substantially revised for the 1982 edition.

© Alfred P. Morgan 1948
Copyright renewed © Ruth S. Morgan 1976
Revised edition © Jack Hill 1982

All rights reserved. No part of this
publication may be reproduced, stored
in a retrieval system, or transmitted,
in any form or by any means, electronic,
mechanical, photocopying, recording or
otherwise, without the prior permission
of David & Charles (Publishers) Limited

Typeset by Keyspools Ltd, Golborne, Lancs
and printed in Great Britain
by Redwood Burn Limited, Trowbridge, Wilts
for David & Charles (Publishers) Limited
Brunel House, Newton Abbot, Devon

Contents

Introduction   7

From the Original Introductory Chapter   9

1 Measuring and Marking Out   11

2 Saws and Sawing   22

3 Planes and Planing   40

4 Chisels and Chiselling   59

5 Hammers and Nails   77

6 Screws and Screwdrivers   93

7 Adhesives and Their Use   110

8 Drills and Drilling   123

9 Power Tools and Attachments   137

10 Smoothing and Finishing   151

11 Tool Sharpening   163

Index   189

Introduction

The prime objective of this book is to help people help themselves. Do-it-yourself and self-sufficiency, together with the increase in leisure time, thanks to advancing technology or whatever, have made the acquisition of woodworking skills a necessity for some and a growing desire of many. Knowing which tools to choose and how to use them properly when you get them is the first step in acquiring such skills. And using the right tool correctly includes keeping it in good working order so that it is able to do its job efficiently.

The old adage 'a bad workman always blames his tools' has a certain ring of truth about it. Even a good workman would have trouble using a screwdriver to do a job which should be done with a chisel or if using a blunt chisel to do the job. But then the really good workman would not use a screwdriver or a blunt chisel, would he? The right tool for the job *is* important and keeping tools in good order *does* matter. This book will help eliminate error and, hopefully, remove the need to blame anyone or anything. It should prove useful to both the complete beginner and the enthusiastic amateur, while even the odd expert here and there may discover where he has been going wrong!

Much of what the book contains was originally written and drawn, in America, by Alfred P. Morgan over thirty years ago. It has been my pleasure to rewrite and rearrange the text, omitting tools and techniques no longer in common use and to update certain sections where required. Some of the illustrations have been redrawn or new ones added and a completely new chapter on small power tools has been added.

INTRODUCTION

In keeping with the perplexities of ways of measuring, imperial measurements are followed by their nearest metric equivalent (in millimetres).

Jack Hill
1982

From the Original Introductory Chapter

Civilization's progress is told in the story of its tools. Primitive man used a few clumsy tools made of stone. We are fortunate in the possession of ingenious and efficient implements of fine steel which extend the force and abilities of our hands ... Without our hammers, chisels, drills, saws ... etc., our living standards would be those of the cave-man ...

Human beings are blessed with ten strong, amazingly dextrous fingers and a world filled with raw materials from which can be fashioned almost anything that may be desired. But fingers alone cannot cut wood and metal and stone. Not much progress can be made in driving a nail with the fist. It is obvious that hands, even though they are guided by an ingenious brain, must have tools to accomplish much.

Anyone possessed of ordinary coordination can easily learn to handle tools efficiently. It is not difficult to use, or to learn how to use, most of the ordinary tools with skill. Do not be dismayed by the dexterity of a skilled workman. Proper instruction and practice will make you skilful also.

First, you must understand the tools you propose to use, their purposes and limitations; then, the proper way to hold them and apply them to the work.

To get the most out of a tool, we do not, for example, pick up a hammer and merely whack at a nail with it or push a saw back and forth to cut wood. We learn the *technique* of using each tool. Starting right is half the secret. If we start right, we soon acquire skill by practising. If we start wrong, practice will not bring skill. Striking a blow is not all there is to using a hammer. There can be artistry in its use or in the use of a saw . . . a screwdriver, a plane, or in fact of any other tool. The skilled craftsman is skilled in the use of his tools because he knows more about his tools than the novice and has learned the technique of using them. His tools have become extensions of his hands and brain.

Alfred P. Morgan
1948

1
Measuring and Marking Out

Cutting wood to exact dimensions is the basis of all good woodworking. Chisels, planes, saws etc are only a means to this end. Before any accurate cutting process can be undertaken successfully, guiding lines must be marked upon the work. The plan and measurements for the work may be taken from a blueprint or sketch, or they may exist only in the mind of the workman. But in either case, a full-sized reproduction of the various angles, curves and details of the plan must be marked on the timber which is the raw material. This measuring and marking process is called 'marking out', 'laying out' or 'setting out'. It is absolutely essential to a good piece of work. In an industrial woodworking workshop this stage of the work is usually carried out by the foreman or another skilled craftsman.

The tools used for marking out are rules, squares, sliding 'T' bevels, gauges, dividers, pencils and marking knives.

Rules

The rules or rulers used by woodworkers are usually of the folding type so that they can be carried in a pocket. They are from 2ft (610mm) to 8ft (2,440mm) long and are usually graduated to show feet, inches and fractions of an inch. Alternatively they may give metric measurements and be graduated in metres, centimetres and millimetres. They are also available with inch divisions on one side and metric divisions on the other. The best are made from boxwood.

The steel tape is also very popular now. This push-pull tape has a flexible steel blade which becomes rigid when

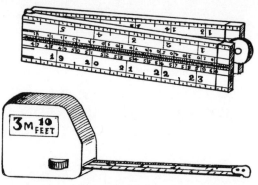

Folding wooden rule and flexible steel tape

extended. Fitted with a hook end this is a useful tool for large-scale work but is not recommended for fine cabinet work. The 12in (305mm) steel rule is often used for accurate work.

Using a Rule

To measure distances of more than 2ft (610mm) the folding rule is laid flat on the surface to be measured. When the rule is laid on a flat surface the rule itself is flat and therefore accurate. It is inaccurate to measure any great length with a folding rule held in the hand; since the rule is flexible, to hold it perfectly straight in this way is difficult.

When marking out accurate measurements of less than 1ft (305mm) the folding rule may be used on its edge or a steel rule used, and the distances marked with a fine pencil point or the tip of a marking knife.

Rules which have been in use for some time are occasionally worn at the ends. In this case it may be more accurate to measure from the 1in or the 10mm mark.

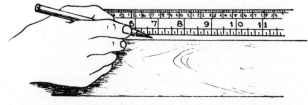

A rule is held on its edge for accurate measurements

Squares

Carpenters' Squares

The largest square is the carpenter's steel square which usually measures about 24in × 18in (610mm × 457mm). The 24in (610mm) side is called the body, and the 18in (457mm) side, at right angles to the body, is called the tongue. The flat sides of the body and tongue are graduated in inches and fractions of an inch or in metric measurements. Both the body and the tongue may be used as a rule and also as a straight edge.

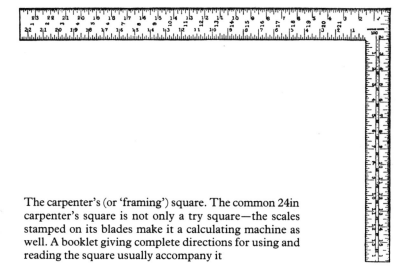

The carpenter's (or 'framing') square. The common 24in carpenter's square is not only a try square—the scales stamped on its blades make it a calculating machine as well. A booklet giving complete directions for using and reading the square usually accompany it

Besides the inch or metric graduations on the square a number of useful tables are marked on it. This square is in fact as important a tool to the carpenter as the slide rule is to the engineer. He performs many of his calculations with the aid of the graduations and tables marked on it and uses it to lay out the guide lines for rafters, oblique joints, stairs etc. In fact, the carpenter's square can be employed in so many different ways that whole books are devoted to its various uses.

The cabinet-maker, joiner and amateur craftsman have little or no use for the tables on a carpenter's square. They use it for laying out and squaring up large pieces of wood and for testing the flatness and squareness of large surfaces. In their hands it is handled much like its smaller brother, the try square.

Try Squares

A try square is a necessity in the woodworker's tool kit. It is used constantly for marking out, and to determine whether edges and ends are true with adjoining edges and with the face of the work after it has been sawn, planed or chiselled.

The common try square consists of two parts at right angles to each other, a thick wood or iron stock and a thin steel blade. Some try squares are made with blades graduated in inches or with a metric scale. The blade length may vary from 4in (100mm) to 12in (305mm).

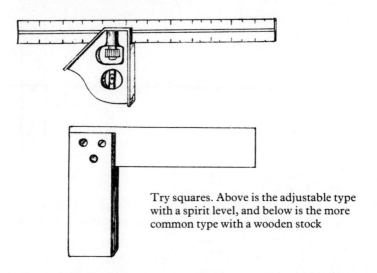

Try squares. Above is the adjustable type with a spirit level, and below is the more common type with a wooden stock

A more expensive form of try square is the adjustable type whose blade can be locked in position at any point along its length. The iron stock is provided with a spirit level.

Marking out with the Square

Pencil versus knife. A pencil is satisfactory for making guide lines for roughing out work. But because of the wide, relatively indefinite mark which it produces, it cannot always be used to lay out the accurate lines required in fine cabinet work, jointing etc. Such work should be marked out with the blade of a pocket knife or a bench or marking knife. The tip of the blade should be used; this makes a clean, accurate line for the meeting sides of joints. Dovetail joints in particular should be marked out with a sharp knife.

Squaring Lines across a Board

When a board is to be cut off, planed or chiselled square, a guide line must be marked across its surface. The guide line must be exactly at the required point and must be square with the edges. A try square is used for this purpose. The stock of the square is pressed firmly against the edge of the board with the left hand and the guide line marked along the blade with a pencil or knife.

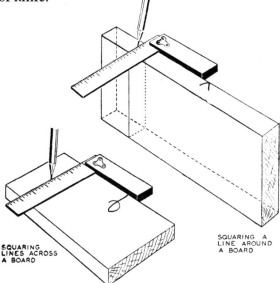

SQUARING A
LINE AROUND
A BOARD

SQUARING
LINES ACROSS
A BOARD

Squaring. The stock of the try square is always placed against the face side or face edge (shown here marked by the conventional symbols)

15

Squaring a Line around a Board

Either a carpenter's square or a try square may be used depending upon the width of the board. The blade of the square should be long enough to reach all the way across the board. Select and mark one square edge and one square side of the board using the conventional face-edge and face-side marks so that they can readily be distinguished as the working edge and working face from which and upon which all measurements are made. Square a line from the face edge across the face side by holding the stock of the try square firmly against the face edge and marking a line along the blade. Lines are then squared from the face side across both edges and from the face edge again across the side of the board opposite the face side.

Sliding 'T' Bevels

The sliding 'T' bevel is a try square which can be adjusted to any angle. It is used for marking out angles other than right angles and for testing bevels. A bevel is any edge not at right angles to the face of a piece of wood.

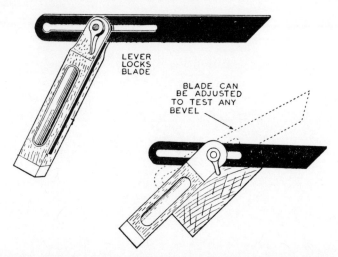

LEVER
LOCKS
BLADE

BLADE CAN
BE ADJUSTED
TO TEST ANY
BEVEL

The sliding 'T' bevel for laying out and testing bevels and angles

Gauging

Gauging is a term used by woodworkers to mean the marking of guide lines parallel to an edge, end or surface of a piece of wood. A good example of gauging is the marking of guide lines for planing etc.

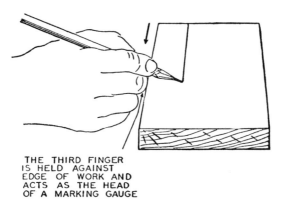

THE THIRD FINGER
IS HELD AGAINST
EDGE OF WORK AND
ACTS AS THE HEAD
OF A MARKING GAUGE

Gauging and marking with a pencil

Gauging with a Pencil
When a not too precise guide line is to be drawn less than 1in (25mm) from an edge, a pencil and the fingers may be substituted for the tool called a marking gauge.

Suppose a guide line for a chamfer is to be gauged on a board $\frac{3}{8}$in (10mm) from its edge. First make a locating mark $\frac{3}{8}$in (10mm) from the edge. Then grasp the pencil near its point with thumb and first and second fingers of the right hand and hold it at an angle of about 30° to the surface to be marked. The tip of the third finger rests against the edge of the wood and acts as a guide in keeping the pencil mark parallel to the edge. The line may be gauged by pushing the pencil either away from the worker or towards him but the angle of the pencil must be kept constant to keep the line parallel to the edge.

When accuracy is not an important consideration for lines gauged more than 1in (25mm) from an edge, a pencil and rule

17

may be used. The point of the pencil is held against the end of the rule with the right hand. The rule is held between thumb and forefinger of the left hand with the second finger against the edge of the wood as a guide. Both hands are moved in unison when the line is drawn.

Marking Gauges

A marking gauge is used for gauging when accuracy is necessary. The tool, made of either wood or metal, consists of

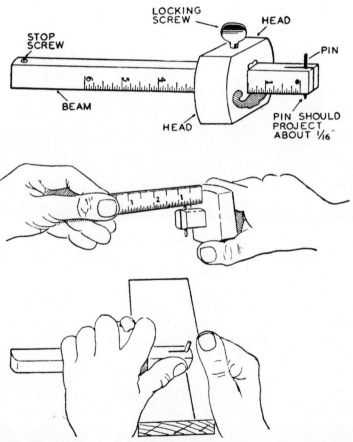

The marking gauge—a tool for marking lines parallel to an edge or making marks at equal distances from an edge or end

a beam about 8in (203mm) long, on which slides a head. The head can be fastened at any point on the beam by means of a thumbscrew on the head. The thumbscrew presses down tightly against the beam and locks it firmly in position. When the gauge is used, a sharpened steel pin or spur cuts the gauge line on the wood. The spur is adjustable; it should project about $\frac{1}{16}$in (1·5mm) and be filed and kept sharp so that it scores the wood like the point of a penknife blade.

A marking gauge must be adjusted by setting the head the proper distance from the point of the spur. Although the beam of a marking gauge may be graduated, the spur may work loose or bend, thus calibrating inaccurately. Consequently, the careful workman pays no attention to the calibrations but sets his gauge by measuring between head and spur.

To draw a line after the gauge has been properly set, grasp the head with palm and fingers of the right or left hand in much the same manner as you would a ball. Extend the thumb along the beam towards the spur. Press the head firmly against the face edge of the piece to be marked and with a wrist motion tip it forward slightly until the spur just touches the wood. The line is made by pushing the gauge away from the worker while keeping the head firmly against the edge of the work all the time. All gauging is done from the face edge or face side.

Mortice Gauges
A mortice gauge is a marking gauge with two spurs. It is used chiefly for laying out mortice and tenon joints. The two spurs mark two parallel lines, the distance between which can be changed by moving one of the spurs controlled by an adjusting screw at the end of the beam. The two spurs are first set the proper distance apart. Then the head is set at the correct distance from them. The mortice gauge is then used in the same manner as the marking gauge.

Many mortice gauges are made with a single spur on the side of the bar opposite the one bearing the two spurs. This

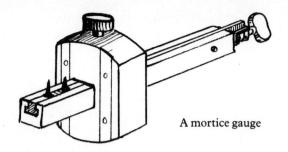

A mortice gauge

makes a dual purpose tool, for, turned over, the mortice gauge can be used as an ordinary marking gauge.

Dividers

Dividers or compasses are used primarily to mark arcs and circles. They can also be used to transfer measurements and to 'step off' equal divisions along a line. There are several types: spring, wing or 'firm joint', the name describing the way in which the legs of the tool are held apart when in use. Dividers generally have metal tips to both legs. Others have a pencil point on one side similar to a drawing compass.

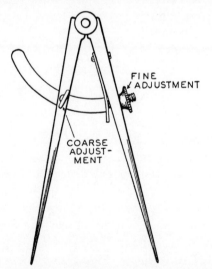

FINE ADJUSTMENT

COARSE ADJUST-MENT

Dividers—used for laying out circles or parts of circles and for picking up distances to be transferred to the work

Pencils and Marking Knives

Brief mention has already been made of these. Pencils should be of medium HB grade and kept properly sharpened. Too much pressure on too fine a point will result in breakage. Special 'carpenters' pencils' which have a broad flat 'lead' are available for laying out rough or large-scale work. Marking knives, sometimes called bench knives, have a short blade ground on one side only. The flat side is run against the blade of the try square when marking out. The knife, held like a pencil, is drawn firmly across the wood so as to leave a clean cut, square on the finished side of the work and bevelled on the waste side. The knife should be kept sharp.

2

Saws and Sawing

Practically everyone is familiar with the standard hand saw. Some will consider it presumptuous to tell them how to saw as it would be to tell them how to walk or run. But whereas walking may consist of moving your legs back and forth, sawing is not merely pushing a saw back and forth. You can cut good firewood that way, but to cut wood accurately you have to use your eye and your head as well as your muscles. Accurate sawing requires a knack which is acquired by knowledge and practice. When you have the knack, it is easy to cut a piece of 10in (254mm) timber to accurate length and find upon checking it with a try square that the end is at 90° with the top, bottom and sides.

The Right Saw for the Job
The wooden portion you grip in your hand when sawing is the handle. The toothed steel portion which extends from the handle and which does the sawing is the blade. To the skilled craftsman there is only one saw intended for each specific job. The stair maker and the boat builder each use special saws in their work which neither the carpenter nor the ordinary woodworker needs. The correct tool always makes work easier; it saves time and energy and produces better results.

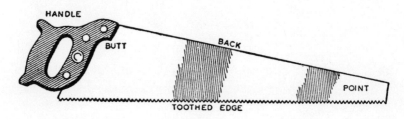

The 'grain of the wood' must be taken into consideration in all woodworking operations. All wood has grain, and the same saw will not cut equally well across the grain and with the grain. Therefore, there are two main types of hand saw for wood. One, called a rip saw, is made to saw in the direction of the grain, usually lengthways along a piece of wood. The other, called a cross-cut saw, is used for cutting across the grain.

CROSS-CUT

RIP

Cross-cut and rip saws. By examining the teeth you can distinguish between a cross-cut saw (for cutting across the grain) and a rip saw (for cutting with the grain). The teeth of a cross-cut saw are sharpened at a bevel so that they are pointed like the end of a knife blade. The teeth of a rip saw are sharpened like chisels

You can distinguish between a rip saw and a cross-cut by examining the teeth. A rip saw usually has larger teeth than a cross-cut of the same length, but it is the manner in which the teeth are set and sharpened which is their most important difference. In both types the teeth are set alternately to left and right so as to form a kerf (the slot which the saw forms as it cuts) which is wider than the thickness of the blade. The teeth on a rip saw are given less set than the teeth on a cross-cut. If you look closely at them you will see that they are shaped like chisels. In fact, they cut wood exactly like a gang of small vertical chisels arranged in a row.

The teeth of a cross-cut saw are sharpened at a bevel so that they are pointed like a knife blade. This provides two lines of sharp points which cut across the wood fibres like knives. The teeth then force out the wood between the two cuts.

23

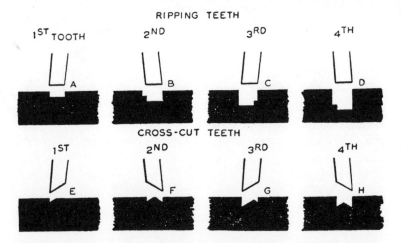

RIPPING TEETH

1ST TOOTH   2ND   3RD   4TH

A   B   C   D

CROSS-CUT TEETH

1ST   2ND   3RD   4TH

E   F   G   H

How saw teeth cut. The teeth of a cross-cut saw first cut across the fibres, then remove the wood. If the first tooth which strikes the wood is set to the left, the point will cut across the fibres and make an incision as at E in the illustration. The following tooth will cut across the fibres to the right as at F. The teeth which follow deepen the incisions and chisel out the wood as shown by G and H.

When a cut is made with a rip saw, if the first tooth striking the wood is set to the left, it will make a groove as shown at A. The next tooth will enlarge the groove as shown at B. The following teeth will make the groove deeper as shown at C and D

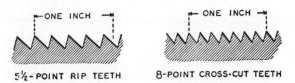

5½-POINT RIP TEETH   8-POINT CROSS-CUT TEETH

The size of the saw teeth. The term 'points to the inch' indicates the size of the teeth. For ordinary cross-cut work a 6- or 8-point saw is used, but for finer work 10 or 12 points are better. A rip saw having $5\frac{1}{2}$ points to the inch will cut rapidly and easily in pine and other softwoods. For ripping oak, cherry, mahogany and other hardwoods, a 6- or 7-point saw is most satisfactory

There are four common sizes of hand saw. The size is the length of the toothed edge measured in inches. The most popular sizes are 24in (610mm) and 26in (660mm).

The coarseness or fineness of a saw depends upon the size of the teeth and is designated by the number of tooth points per inch. The saw having few teeth—5, 5½, 6 or 7 points per inch—will cut fast but make a rough cut. Rip saws are usually in this category. The common hand cross-cut saw can be obtained with 8, 9, 10, 11 or 12 points per inch.

A short (20in (507mm) or less) cross-cut saw with 12 points to the inch and known generally as a panel saw is particularly suitable for sawing plywood sheet. Keep it at a low sawing angle to prevent 'tearing' on the underside of the sheet.

Green or wet wood can best be cut across grain with coarse teeth (6 or 7 points per inch (25mm)) having a wide set. Dry, seasoned wood requires finer teeth (10 or 11 points per inch (25mm)) with a narrow set. A fine-tooth saw is better for smooth accurate cutting.

For general work a 24in (610mm) or 26in (660mm) rip saw with 5½ or 6 points to the inch (25mm) and a 24in (610mm) cross-cut with 8 or 9 points to the inch (25mm) are most widely used.

Quality saws are taper ground so that the steel blade is thinner at the back than at the toothed edge. A tapered blade makes a saw easier to push back and forth in the kerf.

The Care of a Saw
Moisture on the blade of a saw, unless the surface is well protected by a thin film of oil, produces rust almost immediately. Rust will pit and roughen the smooth sides of a saw blade. In order for a saw to be in perfect working condition both sides of the blade must be smooth. At the first sign of any rust spots on a saw blade, rub them off with wire wool or fine emery cloth and apply a coat of light oil or dry lubricant. Keep your saws in a dry place and hang them up when not in use. An unoiled saw blade will rust if it is not used regularly. When you lay down a saw do so carefully. Do not place things on top of it on the bench, never leave it on the floor and do not drop it. A dull saw makes hard work of sawing. A saw cuts with ease when properly sharpened and set. Keep it that way. Instructions for sharpening and setting are given in chapter 11.

Sawing

Before a piece of wood can be sawn to accurate size or shape, it must be marked with a line which will serve as a guide for the saw cut. Rough work can be marked with a pencil. Use a try square as a guide for the pencil if the cut is to be made at right angles and a sliding 'T' bevel if the cut is to be made at an angle other than 90°.

A pencil line is easy to see, but when drawn on wood it may sometimes be too thick for close work. For accurate or small work the mark should be made with the marking knife as described in the previous chapter. A marking or mortice gauge is frequently used in laying out work for sawing, especially when making a mortice, a tenon or a rebate.

In sawing, allowance must be made for the width of the saw cut or kerf. Do not saw directly on the marked line. Accurate sawing is always done on the waste side of the line leaving the marked line showing. Sawing on the line or on the wrong side of the line makes the piece too short. If you leave too much wood it can be planed or chiselled off. But if you leave too little, there is no 'putting on tool' which will put it back. When several pieces are to be cut from a long board, each should be marked out and sawn separately on the waste side. If all are marked out at the same time, an allowance must be made for the kerf between each piece. About $\frac{1}{8}$in (3mm) is generally sufficient.

How to Use a Cross-cut Saw
Start the kerf by drawing the saw backwards across an edge of the timber on the waste side of the line. Guide the blade carefully with the tip or the first joint of the left thumb, bearing in mind that if you are careless you may cut yourself. In cross cutting, a 45° angle between the saw and the work will give best results. It may be necessary to draw the saw back two or three times before the kerf will be properly started. Continue to guide it with your thumb so that the kerf is started at the exact point where you wish the cut to begin.

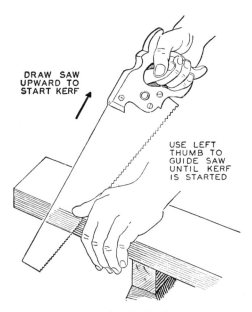

DRAW SAW
UPWARD TO
START KERF

USE LEFT
THUMB TO
GUIDE SAW
UNTIL KERF
IS STARTED

Starting the kerf

Draw the blade back slowly. A too rapid motion will cause the saw to jump, starting the kerf in the wrong place, and perhaps will give you a sore thumb.

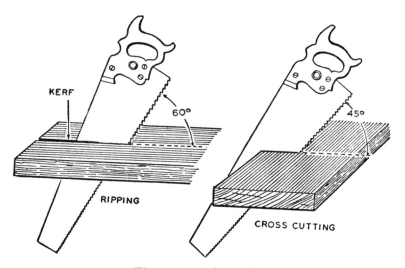

KERF

60°

RIPPING

45°

CROSS CUTTING

The correct sawing angles

27

How to Use a Rip Saw

If the rip saw is a coarse one, it will have a few fine teeth at the end furthest from the handle; this end, incidentally, is usually referred to as the point of the saw. The cut should be started with the fine teeth at the point of the saw by drawing them back several times in the manner already described for starting the cross-cut saw. When ripping, an angle of about 60° between the blade and the work gives the best results. The teeth of either saw will cut most efficiently only when the blade is held approximately at the angles suggested.

Hints for Sawing

The piece to be sawn must be held firmly in a vice, or on a workbench, a box or a pair of saw horses (small trestles made for this purpose). Small work can often be held firmly on a bench or table by the pressure of the left hand or by use of a suitable bench hook (see diagram). Pieces of considerable

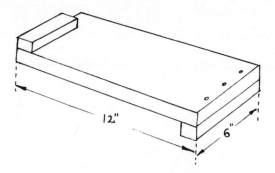

An easily made bench hook

length are best supported on a pair of saw horses, or on two boxes or two old chairs and held firmly by the pressure of one knee. Sometimes, assistance may be required to hold the work really steady.

As the saw progresses across the grain of a board, the weight of the board tends to close the cut and bind the saw so that you can no longer push the blade back and forth. If the waste end is a short, light piece, you can hold it up with your left hand while sawing and prevent the slot from closing on the blade. You will need an assistant to hold a long or heavy piece. Moreover, if you do not support the waste end properly, it will break off just as you are finishing the cut and take a long splinter from the bottom corner of the other piece with it. Gluing the splinter back in place is no substitute for avoiding this problem.

The proper position and grip for sawing permits long easy strokes using nearly the full length of the blade. Take your time and be careful not to jerk the saw back and forth. It is difficult to keep the kerf beside the marked line where it belongs if much of the cutting is done with only a few inches of the blade.

Watch your grip on the handle closely when you are learning to saw. It should be firm but not tight. The saw should run freely. A tight grip prevents the free running of the saw and tends to swerve the blade away from the line. The thumb should be against the left side of the handle, the index finger extended along the right side to help guide the blade. If the blade starts to cut into the marked line or to move too far away from it, twist the handle slightly in order to bring it back to the correct position.

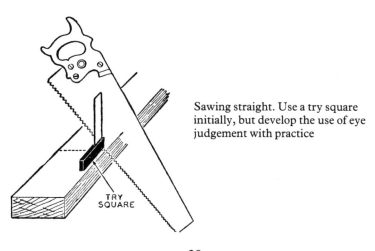

Sawing straight. Use a try square initially, but develop the use of eye judgement with practice

29

To keep the saw at right angles to the surface of the work is the most difficult thing to learn in sawing. The beginner should make an occasional test with a try square to check that the saw is in a perfectly vertical position to help develop the knack of sawing square. Check the position of the blade in this way from time to time until the tests show that you can get along without doing it. That stage in your skill will not be reached the first few times that you use a saw. It will come only with careful practice. Accurate sawing is done with long, easy, relaxed strokes, guided by hand and eye, and is mastered only with practice.

All the cutting action of the teeth on a hand saw takes place on the forward or pushing stroke of the saw blade. Do not try to make the teeth cut on the backward or pulling stroke. Relax and lift it more than pull it. If the tip of the blade vibrates when the blade is brought back on the return stroke, you are not allowing the saw to run freely but are bending or twisting it slightly.

Look carefully for nails in the path of the saw when second-hand timber is used or repair work is done. A hand saw will not cut nails. If it is drawn or pushed over a nail, the sharp points and edges will be knocked off the teeth. And one final, simple point: remember to keep on blowing the sawdust away so that the guide line is not obscured.

Back Saws

A back saw is a thin-bladed cross-cut saw with fine teeth, stiffened by a thick rib of steel or, in better quality saws, brass, along the back edge. Back saws are used for accurate bench work and joint cutting. The work is held either by a bench hook or in the vice. There are two main types of back saw, known usually as tenon saws and dovetail saws. Large tenon saws may be known as mitre box saws and some dovetail saws as light back saws or beading saws.

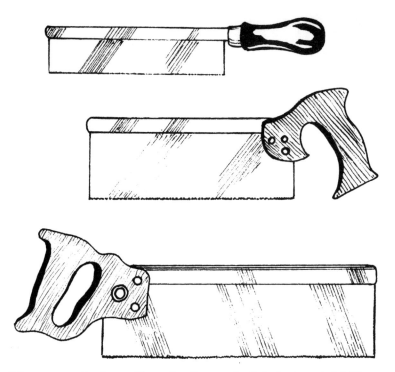

Three types of back saw. Top, a beading saw (or light back saw). Middle, a dovetail saw. Bottom, a typical tenon saw

Tenon Saws

These range in size from a blade length of 8in (203mm) with 16 points to the inch to a blade length of 16in (406mm) with 12 points to the inch. A popular size for fairly smooth accurate cutting is the 10in (254mm) or 12in (305mm) with 14 points to the inch. Larger saws, with blade lengths of up to 24in (610mm) are made for use with a mitre box or jig. This acts as a guide for the saw blade, holding it at the proper angle to make either square or 45° cuts accurately. The simplest form of mitre box is made of three pieces of wood fastened together to form a trough, open at the top and both ends (see diagram). It has several slots in the sides which form saw guides. To saw off a piece of wood square or at an angle of 45° in a mitre box, put the work in position in the box so that the cut to be made lines up with the correct slots in the box. Hold the work firmly

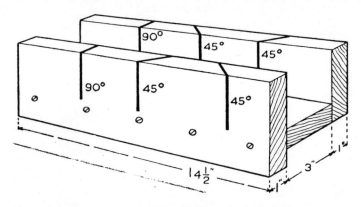

A home-made mitre box. The front of the box projects below the bottom so that it can be hooked against the front edge of the workbench

against the bottom and the back of the box as shown in the diagram. Place the saw in the slot and start the cut slowly and carefully, using the back stroke and holding the handle of the saw upwards until the kerf is established. Then begin sawing, gradually lower the handle until the blade is horizontal and complete the cut with it in that position.

A number of commercially produced sawing aids for cutting mitres etc are available. Most can be used with the more popular sizes of tenon saw.

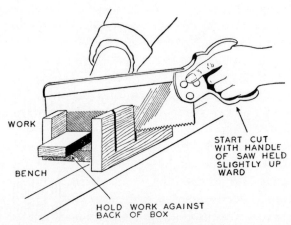

Using a back saw and mitre box

32

Dovetail Saws
Similar to but smaller than the tenon saw, these range in size from 6in (152mm) to 10in (254mm) with from 18 to 22 points per inch (25mm). For fine, accurate work these saws are particularly suitable for cutting dovetail joints as the name implies. The light back saw or beading saw has a plain round handle in line with the back rib. It can be used for small dovetails but is more suitable for cutting mouldings, model making etc.

Using a Back Saw
The woodworking beginner who will carefully practise with a back saw can learn to use these tools with some skill in only a few hours.

The guide line for sawing with a back saw should always be scored with a marking knife or gauge. A pencil line is not really fine enough for the accurate work which can be done with a back saw. Good exercise for practising with a back saw is to cut thin sections from the end of a block of wood. Take a block of softwood about 2in (50mm) square and about 12in (305mm) long. Mark it out as shown in the illustration by scoring lines with a knife and a try square on the front, upper and back surfaces. The lines should be about $\frac{1}{4}$in (6mm) apart; these are the guide lines for cutting the sections. The left hand grips the wood to the bench hook and the thumb of that hand guides the saw in starting the saw cut on the far edge of the wood. In starting the cut, the handle of the saw is drawn up and backwards to begin with. With the kerf established the saw is pushed forward and, as the cut progresses, is lowered gradually to a horizontal position. The saw cut through the block should be true to each of the three lines and the kerf should be close to but just outside the knife line. If the sawing is done accurately, the saw teeth should not scratch any of the knife cuts but, at the same time, should be so close that there is no wood left projecting beyond the mark.

A simple trick which will aid in getting a back saw started so as to make a straight and accurate cut is to cut a triangular

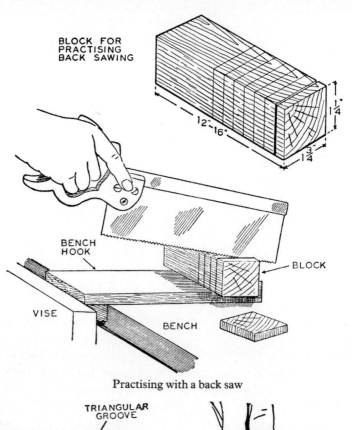

BLOCK FOR
PRACTISING
BACK SAWING

1¼"

¾"

12"-16"

BENCH
HOOK

VISE

BLOCK

BENCH

Practising with a back saw

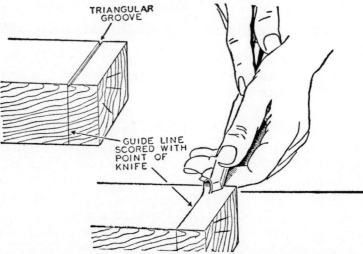

TRIANGULAR
GROOVE

GUIDE LINE
SCORED WITH
POINT OF
KNIFE

To help secure a straight and accurate cut with a back saw, cut a triangular groove on the waste side of the scored line. Start the saw in the groove

groove on the waste side of the scored line. The cut can be made with a chisel as shown.

Compass Saws

The narrow tapered blade of a compass saw is used for cutting large curves or holes in wood. In the latter instance a hole must first be drilled through the wood to start the saw blade. Compass saws come with either a fixed blade or a removable blade which can be used in reversed position for under-cutting. The teeth have considerable set so that they cut almost equally well with or across the grain. The blade length varies from 10in (254mm) to 16in (402mm). The teeth usually have 8 or 9 points to the inch (25mm).

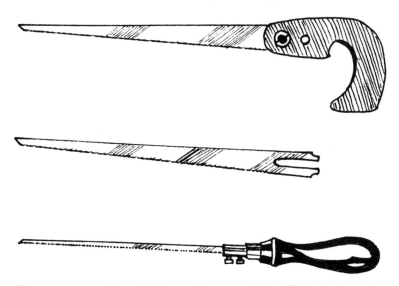

The compass saw (above) is shown with a spare blade. The keyhole saw has a hollow handle

Keyhole Saws

A keyhole saw, also known as a pad saw, is similar to a compass saw but smaller. It is used in the same way. Usually, it has a round handle in line with the blade. Its 10in (254mm) or 12in (305mm) removable blade with 10 points to the inch

(25mm) is made very narrow for small work in close quarters, such as cutting keyholes, sharp curves, fretwork etc. The round handle is hollow throughout so that only part of the blade need protrude in awkward corners.

To cut a keyhole in a door or drawer, first mark the outline of the hole in the desired position. Drill a hole through the marked position large enough to pass the blade of the keyhole saw. Then carefully cut along the marked line turning the saw as necessary.

Frame Saws

These saws are for sawing along curved lines, whether concave or convex. For this the blades must be very thin. Support for the thin blade is therefore provided by a tensioned wood or metal frame. Such saws come in several different categories.

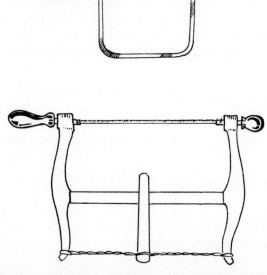

Two frame saws. The larger one is a bow saw and has a wooden frame. The other is a coping saw and has a springy metal frame and a wooden handle

Coping Saws

A coping saw takes narrow, disposable blades which are held in a metal frame fitted with a wooden handle. A coping saw is used to cut curves and intricate patterns in thin wood. Carpenters sometimes use this tool for shaping or 'returning' the ends of wooden mouldings.

It is customary to place the blade in the frame with the teeth pointing towards the handle so that it cuts when the handle is pulled and not when it is pushed. This is of course the opposite of an ordinary hand saw and the arrangement is said to give better control of the small blade. The standard blade which measures 6in (165mm) long is kept under tension by means of a threaded stretcher which is adjusted by turning the handle. The blade is fitted at its ends with pins which slip into slots in the stretcher at each end of the frame. The blade may be turned through 360° to facilitate work on awkward shapes. By lining up the two pegs shown, a twisted blade is avoided. Blades for this saw are made either to cut wood only or to cut wood and a variety of other materials, including plastic and soft metals in sheet form such as copper etc. Round 'blades' which act like a file and can be used to cut in any direction are also available.

Fret Saws

These saws have a larger capacity frame but a shorter and much finer blade than the coping saw. The depth of the frame, ie the space between the blade and the back of the frame, denotes the size of the saw. It is used for cutting curves of all kinds and the delicate patterns known as fretwood in thin wood and plywood up to about $\frac{1}{4}$in (6mm) thick. The blade's fine teeth give a clean cut without splintering.

Both coping saws and fret saws are usually worked with an up and down movement so that the blade moves vertically. The work is supported in this case on a saddle which is held in a vice or screwed to the workbench. A saddle for this purpose is easily made and consists of two boards fastened together to form an 'L' shape as shown. The 'V'-shaped notch is about

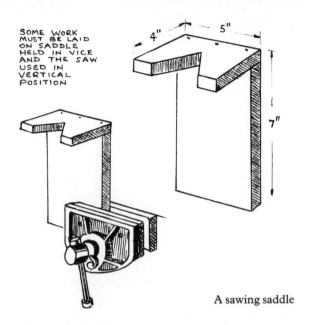

SOME WORK MUST BE LAID ON SADDLE HELD IN VICE AND THE SAW USED IN VERTICAL POSITION

4"   5"

7"

A sawing saddle

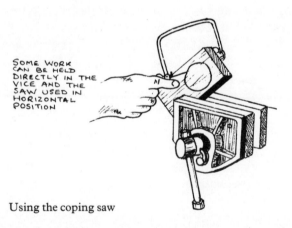

SOME WORK CAN BE HELD DIRECTLY IN THE VICE AND THE SAW USED IN HORIZONTAL POSITION

Using the coping saw

3in (76mm) wide and the same depth. The work to be sawn is marked with the design to be followed by the saw and held on the saddle so that the saw blade can work up and down in the notch. Since the saw is held below the saddle and the cutting done on the down stroke, the work is not lifted from the saddle by the motion of the blade. The work is turned and shifted from time to time to keep the saw blade in the 'V' notch and to accommodate the curves as they are encountered. When using the coping saw, some work can be held directly in the vice and the saw moved horizontally.

Bow Saws

The original frame saws, these have a thin blade held in a wooden frame. Tension is applied to the blade by means of a twisted cord. The disposable blade, with an average length of 12in (305mm), has coarse teeth, and the saw is used for cutting curves in wood $\frac{1}{2}$in (12mm) thick and more. As with the coping saw the blade may be rotated in the frame.

The narrow blades of all types of frame saw make them rather difficult to control at first. Keep to the waste side of the line and let the blade run freely in the kerf without binding. With practice, accurate curved cuts will be made.

3
Planes and Planing

There is something fascinating about the sound of a plane and the manner in which the shavings curl out of it. The fresh, pleasant smell of wood rises to your nostrils. Almost everyone who has watched a carpenter using a plane has had an urge to get his own hands on the tool and make his own shavings.

However, the technique of planing involves more than just making shavings. Know-how is necessary. It is necessary to know how to adjust, how to hold and how to push one of these indispensable tools in order to produce good workmanship. In principle, a plane is a kind of chisel set in a block of wood or, nowadays, a metal frame which acts as a guide to regulate the angle and depth of cut. A chisel-like plane 'iron' or blade does the cutting. This must have a keen edge and be correctly set, and the whole tool must be properly controlled.

There are several types of plane. Each has a special purpose. The most common are the jack plane and the smoothing plane. Other similar types include the fore and try or jointer planes. All are made on the same principle but differ in size and use.

The general purpose of these planes is to smooth off rough surfaces and bring work to exact size after it has first been roughed out to approximate size. For example, it is not possible to make a close fit with a hand saw alone. A saw does not cut to accurate size and it leaves a rough, uneven surface. But sawn edges can be smoothed with a plane and brought to close dimensions. There are also planes for special purposes, such as block planes, rebate planes, plough planes, circular planes etc. Other planes combine several functions in one tool. All are described in this chapter.

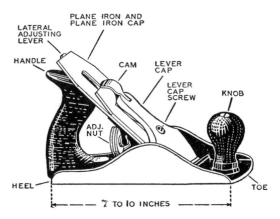

The smoothing plane. This is the shortest of the two-handed planes. It is used to smooth work after unevenness has been removed by a longer plane

Old planes were made with solid hardwood frames. Later, planes made in a combination of wood and metal were introduced. Many of these were beautiful pieces of precision craftsmanship, and those which remain have become coveted collectors' items. The modern plane has an open, cast-iron frame with machined surfaces.

Holding the Work

While being planed, work should be so firmly secured that it cannot move. A skilled woodworker will sometimes hold a short length of board on its edge with one hand and use the other to drive the plane, but that ability comes only with experience. It will be found that the most efficient way to hold the workpiece is to grip it in a bench vice and to treat planing as a two-handed job.

When planing wide boards which will not fit the jaws of the vice, these may be clamped to the bench surface or held up against the bench stop. A bench stop, or hook, is a simple wooden block fitted into a hole at one end of some benches. A thin strip of wood fixed across the end of the bench can also be used as a stop. The ideal holding arrangement is where the vice is fitted with an adjustable dog—a square steel peg (sometimes two steel pegs) and corresponding holes at intervals across the bench surface. This arrangement permits

41

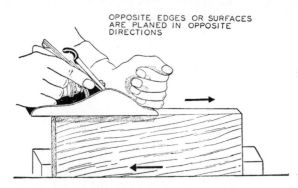

OPPOSITE EDGES OR SURFACES
ARE PLANED IN OPPOSITE
DIRECTIONS

Always plane with the grain. If the grain is torn or roughened by the plane, reverse the direction in which the plane is pushed

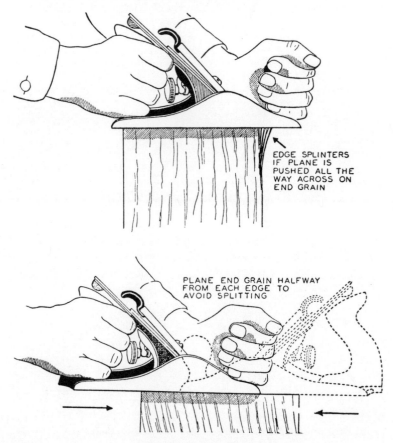

EDGE SPLINTERS
IF PLANE IS
PUSHED ALL THE
WAY ACROSS ON
END GRAIN

PLANE END GRAIN HALFWAY
FROM EACH EDGE TO
AVOID SPLITTING

How to plane end grain

boards to be clamped between the vice dog or dogs and pegs located in suitably spaced holes in the bench.

The Grain of the Wood

As you know, all wood has a grain (the direction in which the fibres run) and the grain seldom runs parallel to the surface. You must take this into consideration when planing. To plane a wood surface smooth it is necessary to plane *with* the grain, not *against* it. If the wood is torn and roughened by a sharp plane set to make thin shavings, you are planing against the grain. Reverse the work and plane from the opposite end. If the grain is irregular, it may be necessary to plane one portion of a surface in one direction and the other portion in the opposite direction. When cross grain or curly grain is encountered, the plane-cutting iron must be very sharp and set to cut a very thin shaving.

It is necessary to plane *end* grain halfway from each edge. If you push a plane all the way across end grain, the far corners or edge will split off. Plane from one edge to just past the centre, then move to the other edge and plane to the centre again. Alternatively there are several tricks which can be used in end planing to avoid breaking corners at the end of the

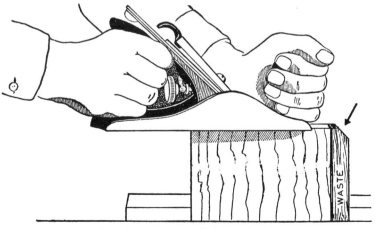

A trick to prevent splitting end grain

43

stroke. One of them is to clamp a piece of waste wood on the edge of the board which is at the end of the plane stroke. This piece should be on the same level as the piece being planed. Any edge splitting will then take place on this waste piece.

Types of Plane

The first few cuts on a long surface require a long plane. The bottom or sole of a long plane covers so much area that it rides over any hollows in the work and cuts only on the high spots until the surface is even. Therefore it is easier to straighten a long edge or surface with a long soled plane than it is with a shorter variety. After the unevenness has been removed with a long plane, the work can be finished off with a smaller plane called a smoothing plane.

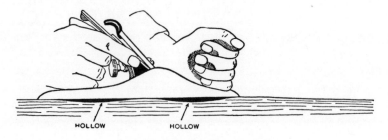

HOLLOW   HOLLOW

The cutting action of a long plane

Jack, Fore and Jointer Planes

Long planes are called jack, fore, try or jointer planes depending upon their length. The sole of a jack plane is usually about 14in (355mm) long; that of a fore plane about 18in (457mm) and on a jointer or try plane from 22in (560mm) to 24in (610mm). Among these the jack plane is used most often. Since all three are alike except for the length of the sole, our discussion of a jack plane will apply equally well to the others.

Planing with a Jack Plane

At the back of a jack plane is a handle somewhat like the

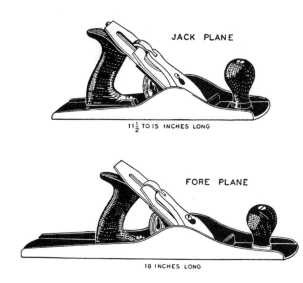

JACK PLANE

$11\frac{1}{2}$ TO 15 INCHES LONG

FORE PLANE

18 INCHES LONG

The smoothing, jack, fore and jointer planes are alike except in length

handle of a saw. An upright knob is fixed forward of the blade. It is obviously a tool to be used with both hands.

If your hand and eye are skilful enough to guide the plane firmly and accurately, you will have no trouble. You may, however, have to practise a great deal before you can plane properly. At the start of the planing stroke take up a position behind the work with the left foot forward and the weight of the body resting on the right foot. As you push the plane forward shift the weight gradually and rhythmically to the left foot. Press down and forward at the beginning of the stroke and maintain the same pressure throughout the forward motion. An even pressure is essential. Beginners are likely to bear down hard at the beginning of a planing stroke, lighten the pressure toward the centre and bear down again at the end. Some do the opposite—bear down harder at the centre than at the ends. The result of both mistakes will be a convex or a concave surface instead of a straight one.

Another common mistake, especially when planing edges, is to allow the plane to rock sideways resulting in a sloping, or worse, a twisted surface. Hold the plane square to the wood throughout each stroke. Practise planing on pieces of scrap wood. Check the work frequently with a try square and straight edge. Planing, like all woodworking, is easy enough if you first master the fundamentals.

Planing with a Smoothing Plane

A smoothing plane is made exactly like a jack plane but with a shorter sole. This may be from about 7in (178mm) to 10in (254mm) in length. It is used to smooth the surface of work after the rough or uneven surface has been removed with a jack plane.

Hold the plane as square as you can while you work, and remember that, since this plane has a short sole, you can quickly make 'hollows' and 'rounds' with it if you do not apply the proper pressure to make an even shaving. Contrary to what has just been said about maintaining an even pressure with the jack plane, the following might be helpful when using a short soled plane.

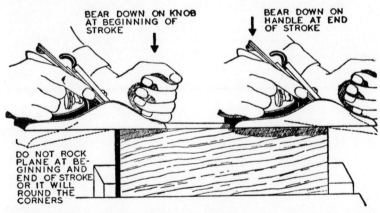

How to produce a shaving of approximately the same thickness from the beginning to the end of the stroke

At the beginning of any stroke, you should put a little more downward pressure on the front knob with your left hand than you do on the handle with your right hand. When the stroke has been started, the pressure of both hands should be equal until towards the end. At the end, all the downward

46

pressure should be exerted on the handle and practically none on the knob. This should result in a shaving of approximately the same thickness from the beginning to the end of the stroke.

It does not take much planing to dull a keen edge on a plane blade (usually known as the cutting iron or simply the iron). You should be able to sharpen your own plane. Complete instructions for removing the blade, grinding and honing are given in chapter 11. Even with a sharp blade, correct adjustment of the plane is also very important.

How to Adjust a Plane

The jack, fore, jointer and smoothing planes each have a plane iron cap, the cap iron, clamped to the cutting iron. This has a double purpose. It stiffens the cutting iron, and breaks and curls the shavings as they come up through the throat of the plane. The breaking and curling and the action of the toe (the portion of the sole forward of the throat) prevent the wood from splitting ahead of the cutting edge and are the reasons for the cutting edge producing a smooth surface. Cap iron and cutting iron are secured in the plane by the lever cap.

The position of the cap iron in relation to the cutting iron is adjustable and can be moved by loosening the cap iron screw.

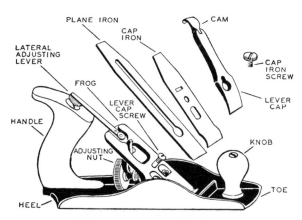

The separate parts of a plane

47

A correct adjustment is essential. For general work the edge of the cap iron should be about $\frac{1}{16}$in (1·5mm) back from the cutting edge of the cutting iron. For softwood it can be a little further back, but for cross grained or curly grained wood it should be as near the cutting edge as possible.

To set the plane, hold it bottom side up in the left hand with the toe of the plane towards you and the sole level with the eye. Sight along the sole and, with the right hand, turn the adjusting nut located just forward of the handle until the sharp edge of the blade projects slightly through the throat and above the sole of the plane. The blade is pushed *out* when the adjusting nut is turned clockwise and moves back towards the handle. Turning the nut anticlockwise so that it moves forward draws the blade *in*.

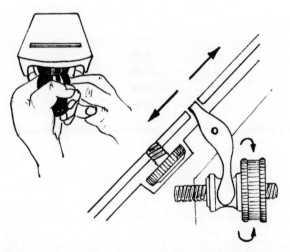

Adjusting the depth of cut on a plane. The adjusting nut is used to raise or lower the blade

The most common mistake made is setting the blade too far out. Only its edge should be visible. You should be able to just feel the edge by moving the ball of the hand very lightly along the sole of the plane. In use, if the blade is sharp and properly set, it will cut thin, even shavings. A thick shaving is not required and only makes the work more difficult to do and the end result unsatisfactory.

The adjustment to regulate the depth of cut is called the vertical adjustment. The plane must also be set so that it makes shavings of even thickness and so that, in planing wide surfaces, one corner of the blade does not 'dig in'. This is done with the lateral adjustment lever. Sight along the sole of the plane and move the lever to right or left as required to make the cutting edge 'square' to the sole.

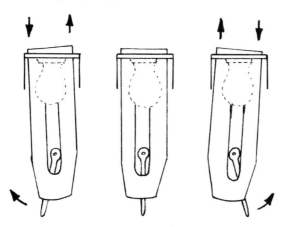

Using the lateral adjustment lever

Cutting irons should be kept sharp. If the throat becomes clogged with shavings, stop planing and clear it immediately. Never use a screwdriver or anything made of metal because it will dull or even nick the cutting edge of the plane iron. A wooden splint may be used if shavings cannot be pulled clear with the fingers.

Special Purpose Planes

Special purpose planes include block planes, filister, rebate or 'rabbet' planes, shoulder, router and plough planes. Combination, multi- and universal planes combine the functions of many of these specialised planes in a single tool and, by making use of an assortment of specially shaped cutters, can be used also as moulding planes etc.

Block Planes
These are used mainly to plane end grain. Because the cutting iron is set at a lower angle than other planes, it will cut end grain better. It is the proper tool to use to make chamfers on small pieces of wood and for planing the ends of mouldings etc.

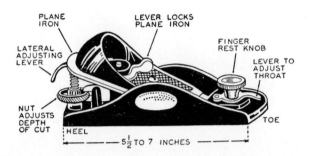

The block plane is the smallest of the common planes. It is used to smooth end grain, make chamfers and shape small pieces of wood

The cutting iron is held in the plane's metal frame by means of a lever cap or a lever cam. The blade does not have a cap iron. Moving the lever-cap screw or the lever cam, whichever the plane may have, in one direction will lock the cutting iron. Moving screw or lever in the opposite direction unlocks the iron so that it can be removed from the frame. The cut of the plane is adjusted by means of an adjusting screw and a lateral adjusting lever. Some block planes have an adjustable throat operated by a small lever at the front of the plane. Cheaper versions of the plane are not fully adjustable. Because of the low angle of the cutting edge of this plane the cutting iron is set in the frame with its bevel *up*.

Holding a Block Plane
One hand only is used to guide and push a block plane. The sides of the plane are grasped between the thumb on one side

and the second and third fingers on the other. The forefinger should be positioned in the hollow of the finger rest at the front of the plane. The lever cap is cradled in the palm of the hand.

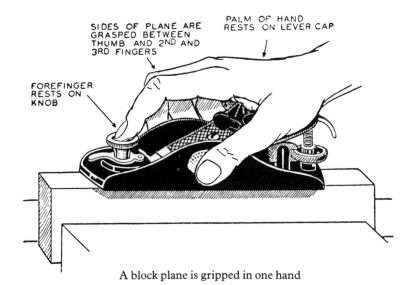

A block plane is gripped in one hand

Rebate Planes

A rectangular recess cut out of the end or edge of a piece of wood is called a rebate or rabbet. Rebates are used to form grooved joints in furniture, doors, windows and box construction etc. They can be cut with a saw and chisel or planed with one of the special planes made for the purpose. Rebate planes are two-handed tools, pushed in the same manner as a smoothing plane or jack plane.

The older-type bench rebate plane is constructed in exactly the same way as a jack or smoothing plane, except that the sole is cut away at the throat so that the cutting iron extends across its full width. This means that the corner of the iron is in line with the side of the plane and cuts right to its edge. In use, a batten is clamped to the workpiece to act as a guide for the side of the plane. The side of the plane is pressed up against

Rebate planes. Above is the older type of bench rebate plane. Below is the improved rebate and filister plane. The former is used up against a batten as shown, whilst the latter incorporates its own guide fence

the batten and worked down to a depth line marked on the edge of the work.

An improved version, sometimes known as the improved rebate and filister plane, has a different-style, all metal body and comes complete with guide fence and depth gauge. The cutting iron can be mounted in two positions: one for normal work and one for 'bull-nose' work, where the plane is required to cut close up to a right angle as in a stopped rebate.

The guide fence slides on one or two detachable arm rods and is held in position with locking screws at the required distance for the width of the rebate. The depth gauge, which is fitted to the opposite side of the plane, is fixed to the required depth measured from the edge of the cutting iron and *not* the sole of the plane.

Using a Rebate Plane

With width and depth settings adjusted or marked, and the work held firmly on the bench, proceed as follows. Rest the plane close to the *far* end of the work and begin by making short cuts out to that end. Keep pressure against the fence or guide batten with the left hand and hold the plane square to the work. Continue making short cutting strokes with the plane, gradually moving backwards as the rebate is established. Repeat this procedure until the marked line is reached or until the depth stop prevents further shavings to be removed. When working a stopped rebate, chisel out the end, change the blade to the forward position of the improved plane and proceed as above.

Shoulder Planes

Shoulder planes are used to trim the shoulders of large joints such as tenons etc. They have a full-width blade as previously described in rebate planes and so can be used to cut right up to the edge of rebates and housings etc. With their narrow blade mounted bevel-uppermost and at a low angle as with the block plane, they can be used for work across end grain.

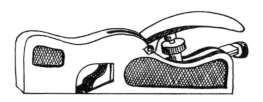

A shoulder plane

There are several types available. All have in common a steel body with machined, parallel sides accurately at right angles to the sole. All have adjusting screws to regulate the depth of cut and most have adjustable throats. Some have detachable noses, which means that the front of the plane can be partly removed to make a bull-nose plane or completely removed so that it can be used as what is known as a chisel plane. This allows the cutting iron to work right up to the end of a stopped rebate.

Using a Shoulder Plane

Because of its machined body the shoulder plane can be used

53

not only in the conventional upright manner but also over on its side. For trimming the shoulders of large tenons the work is clamped flat to the bench and, with the plane on its side and resting on the tenon itself, the shoulder of the joint can be cut true and square. Do not plane through or the edge will split out; work from both sides. Rebates are cut as described previously using a batten as a width guide and planing down carefully to a marked line. For all work the cutting iron should be sharp and set to take a fine shaving.

Routers

The name 'router' is now more readily applied to the portable electric router but the hand router or router plane is a tool used for cutting and cleaning up grooves and recesses in woodwork. It may also be used to accurately level background areas in low relief carving and for cleaning out corners in inlay work.

Its sole is really a flat-base plate to which are fitted two wooden knobs by which it is held. The plane is usually supplied with interchangeable cutters which clamp to a threaded post. The cutters are cranked so that the cutting edge is set at a very shallow angle to the work to produce a chisel-like paring action. In use, the cutter is lowered by means of a knurled nut as the work proceeds until the correct depth is reached. A simple adjustable fence enables the plane to cut grooves parallel to an edge when necessary. A miniature version of the hand router, with a steep angled blade, is known as the 'Old Woman's Tooth'.

Plough Planes

The plough plane is the least elaborate of the type of plane which embraces the combination and multi-plane referred to later. Each consists of a main metal frame or stock into which are screwed two arm bars. These support a sliding section and an adjustable fence.

The plough plane's main use is to cut grooves parallel to an edge, and along the grain of a piece of wood. It can also be used to cut rebates up to about ½in (12mm) in one pass. Wider grooves and rebates can be cut by resetting the fence and making further passes with the plane. The position and depth of the groove to be made are regulated by the setting of the adjustable fence and a depth gauge which attaches to the main body. The width of the groove is determined by the size of blade chosen from the range supplied with the plane.

Using a Plough Plane
A clamp and screw hold the chosen blade or cutter in place. Most blades are adjustable by turning an adjusting screw before tightening the clamp screw. Start at the far end of the work and gradually move back as when using the rebate plane. Work with the grain for a smooth cut, and keep plane and fence hard against and square to the wood. To cut a rebate use a blade slightly wider than the rebate required. Set the fence so that the blade overhangs the rebate's edge. Use as described for grooving.

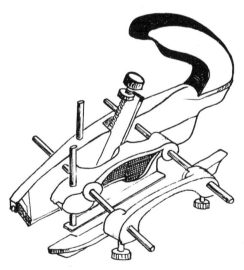

A typical combination or multi-plane. Plough, combination and multi-planes are similar in style, differing mainly in the number of different functions they can perform

Combination and Multi-planes

Similar in general appearance to the plough plane, these tools combine the function of several of the special planes described here.

The combination plane has a stock and sliding section identical with the plough plane. Its main difference lies in spurs, one being fitted to the stock and one to the sliding section. These spurs have knife edges and their function is to cut the wood fibres ahead of the blade, enabling this plane to be used to groove and rebate across the grain. This tool will also cut beads and make tongue-and-groove joints on the edges of boards.

Incorporating features of both the plough plane and the combination plane, the multi-plane can perform an even wider range of functions. By the addition of extra cutters and by replacing the standard sliding section with special bases, a wide range of mouldings can also be cut with the one tool.

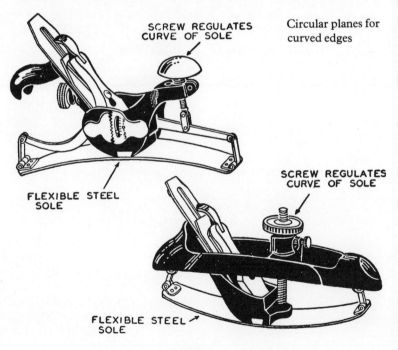

SCREW REGULATES
CURVE OF SOLE

Circular planes for curved edges

FLEXIBLE STEEL
SOLE

SCREW REGULATES
CURVE OF SOLE

FLEXIBLE STEEL
SOLE

56

Compass Planes

Known also as the circular plane, the compass plane will smooth a circular edge, either convex or concave. It has a flexible steel sole which can be adjusted to any radius within the limitations of the plane. The plane uses the same cutter assembly of cutting iron, back iron and lever cap as is fitted to smoothing and jack planes. Setting and adjustment is the same as for these planes, and it is held and used in a similar manner.

Spokeshaves

A spokeshave is not really a plane, but it cuts in the same way and the blade is sharpened the same as a plane cutting iron. It is primarily used to finish curved edges and also for making chamfers. Two types are available, one with a flat sole for convex curves and one with a curved sole for concave curves. The modern spokeshave has a metal stock which is held in both hands. The blade is held in the stock by a cap iron and thumb screw. On the best spokeshaves the blade is adjustable by means of two screws, one on either side, which enable the blade to be finely set both vertically and laterally.

Using a Spokeshave

Hold the spokeshave with both hands, the thumbs on the back edge of the tool to control the angle of cut. The tool is pushed away from you (although some might argue with this) and, to avoid judder and a rippled surface, hold the tool at a slight angle across the wood to make a slicing cut. Always

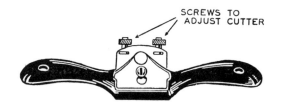

A spokeshave for shaping and smoothing small curves

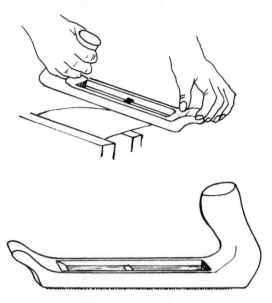

A multi-purpose Surform plane

work in the direction of the grain. Convex curves are cut down each side *from* the centre; concave curves *towards* the centre from each side.

Surform Planes

Again, the Surform plane is not really a plane but a tool used with a planing action to shape wood and other soft materials. Known most often by its trade name, Surform, this tool consists of a light metal frame to which is attached a disposable blade of thin, hardened steel. A series of small teeth, pressed out and ground sharp, form its many cutting edges. Several different types of Surform accept standard-sized blades which may be either curved or flat. These can all be used with or against the grain but, as the cutting action of the blade is rather like that of a coarse rasp, it leaves a rough surface requiring further finishing.

4
Chisels and Chiselling

There are chisels for cutting wood and chisels for cutting metal. Chisels for cutting metal are known as cold chisels and are made from one piece of forged steel, without a handle. Woodworking chisels cannot be used to cut metal and cold chisels are of no value as woodworking tools.

The chisel is one of the most important and most used woodworking tools. It is indispensable in the construction of most wood joints made by hand. The modern wood chisel consists of a blade made from special tool steel, forged and tempered to hold a keen cutting edge, and a handle made from a tough wood, usually beech, hickory or ash, or moulded from high impact plastic. As chisels are frequently in use, only the best quality should be purchased. Although chisels for woodworking are made in several shapes and many sizes to suit the work they perform, they may be divided into two broad categories known as tang and socket chisels. These names tell how the blade and handle are joined together.

Tang Chisels
Generally the blade is secured to the handle by means of a tang—a projecting shank forged on the end of the blade—which fits tightly into a hole in the handle. The handle is reinforced against splitting by means of a metal ferrule. Tang chisels are designed for light work such as paring and carving by hand and will not withstand the over-frequent blows of a heavy mallet. They may be driven with a light-weight wooden or composition mallet without fear of splitting the handle, but primarily they are intended for work in which they are driven by pressure of the hand.

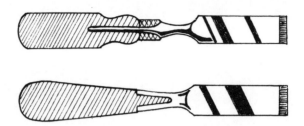

A tang chisel (above) and a socket chisel

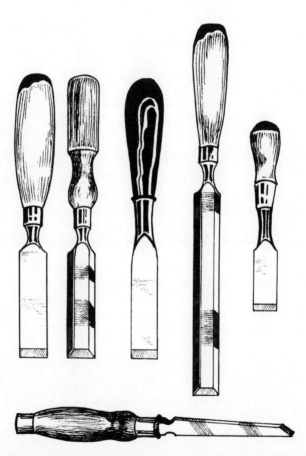

Types of chisel. From left to right: firmer chisel; bevel-edge chisel; high-impact plastic handled firmer chisel; paring chisel; pocket chisel; and (below) mortice chisel

Socket Chisels

For heavier work socket chisels are stronger. One end of the steel blade is formed into a funnel-shaped socket which fits over the tapered end of the handle. The socketed blade is generally thicker than the tanged blade. A range of modern chisels now have high-impact plastic handles moulded into such socketed blades and these are virtually unbreakable. A heavy-duty chisel made to be driven by a steel hammer is also obtainable. A steel-headed hammer is not recommended for driving ordinary wood chisels, however.

Types of Chisel

Differences in the length and shape of the blade give chisels special qualities which make one better adapted to certain work than another. Consequently there are several types of chisel known as firmer, bevel-edge, mortice, paring and butt or pocket chisels whose main difference lies in the shape and proportion of their blades.

Firmer Chisels

These are good general purpose chisels, adaptable for both light and heavy work. They have long, strong blades, rectangular in section.

Bevel-edge Chisels

Preferred by many craftsmen, the bevel-edge chisel is similar in construction to the ordinary firmer chisel except that its blade has its top edges bevelled along its length. This gives it a lighter, thinner blade more suitable for reaching into angles and the corners of joints etc.

Paring Chisels

The blade of a paring chisel is longer, lighter and thinner than the blade of other chisels. It is used mainly for paring and cleaning up joints by hand and should never be struck with a mallet.

61

Butt or Pocket Chisels

These chisels are different from other types only in that they have a shorter blade (usually about 3in (75mm) long when new) and consequently can be used in awkward places inaccessible to a longer blade.

Mortice Chisels

The mortice chisel is used for chiselling mortices and consequently must be driven with a heavy mallet. In chiselling a mortice, the blade is used not only for cutting but also as a lever to force the chips out. Since it receives hard use, the blade of a mortice chisel is made thick and strong just below the handle. Usually mortice chisels are of the socket type—their handles are fitted with a metal ferrule at the top end to protect against splitting. In the case of a tanged tool, a leather washer between the shoulder of the blade and the handle acts as a shock absorber. If a mortice is first bored out so that most of the wood is removed with a drill, it may be cleaned out and squared up with an ordinary firmer or bevel-edge chisel. In that case a special mortice chisel is unnecessary.

Chisel Sizes

Experience will soon teach the workman the most convenient size of chisel to use on a particular job. The chisel should always be smaller than the cut being made. For example, in cutting a recess 1in (25mm) wide in a piece of wood, the chisel used should not be 1in (25mm) wide; a $\frac{1}{2}$in (12mm) is the proper tool to use. The reason for this is that in general a chisel should not be pushed straight forward but moved laterally at the same time as it is pushed forward.

All varieties of chisels are made with blades varying from $\frac{1}{8}$in (3mm) to 1in (25mm) in steps of $\frac{1}{8}$in (3mm) and from 1in (25mm) to 2in (50mm) in steps of $\frac{1}{4}$in (6mm). For most purposes the $\frac{1}{4}$in (6mm), $\frac{1}{2}$in (12mm), $\frac{3}{4}$in (19mm) and 1in (25mm) widths are sufficient. A collection of 9 or 10 chisels which includes perhaps 2 medium-width paring chisels, a $\frac{1}{4}$in

(6mm) or $\frac{1}{2}$in (12mm) mortice chisel, four bevel-edge chisels in the sizes given above, plus one or two of these sizes of firmer chisels, is all that most professional woodworkers need and should satisfy the most particular amateur craftsman.

How to Use a Chisel

You do not gain time by making haste with a chisel. There is always a danger of unintentionally splitting the work by taking too large a cut. Whenever possible, other tools such as saws, planes and drills should be used to remove as much of the waste wood as possible, and the chisel employed for finishing purposes only. This saves both time and effort.

On rough work, the power which drives a chisel is usually the blow of a mallet. On fine work the driving power is applied entirely with the right hand. Most of the control is exercised by the left hand and vice versa in a left-handed person.

It is probably easier to cut yourself accidentally with a chisel than with any other tool, and the cut of a chisel can be wicked. The best safeguard against injury is to hold the tool properly. Keep both hands at the back of the cutting edge at all times. A safety precaution which will not only help to protect the worker but also make the work easier is to always secure the work which is to be chiselled so that it cannot move. Keep chisels sharp at all times. A blunt cutting edge is more likely to be the cause of an accident than a sharp one.

When starting a cut with a chisel, always cut away from the guide line and into the waste wood so that any splitting which takes place will occur in the waste and not on the finished work. Do not start directly on the guide line but slightly away from it so that there is a small amount of material left to be removed by the final finishing cuts. Never cut towards yourself with a chisel, and *never* hold the work with one hand and chisel with the other.

Make the shavings thin, especially when finishing. Examine the grain of the wood to see which way it runs and cut with the grain. This severs the fibres and leaves the wood

63

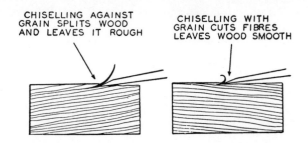

CHISELLING AGAINST
GRAIN SPLITS WOOD
AND LEAVES IT ROUGH

CHISELLING WITH
GRAIN CUTS FIBRES
LEAVES WOOD SMOOTH

Always chisel with the grain to avoid splitting

smooth. Cutting against the grain splits the fibres and leaves the wood rough. Such a cut is also more difficult to control.

Chiselling may be done by cutting either horizontally or vertically. Vertical chiselling cuts are usually made across grain.

Horizontal Chiselling

If the cutting edge of even a well-sharpened chisel is examined under a microscope, it will appear saw-toothed. If, when chiselling, the chisel is pushed directly forward, it will only cut with difficulty. But if the chisel is slanted slightly in the direction of the cut, the minute teeth will cut more easily and smoothly. This sharing cut should be used whenever possible, both with the grain and on end grain. Cutting fine shavings with a sharing cut is called paring.

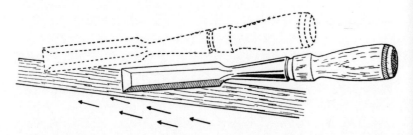

A shearing cut is used when possible. The chisel should be slanted slightly in the direction of the cut and moved slightly sideways as it is pushed forward. The illustration shows a chisel at the start of a horizontal cut. The dotted lines indicate the position of the chisel toward the end of the cut and show that the tool has been moved slightly sideways at the same time it was pushed forward, thus making a shearing cut

64

Cutting Horizontally with the Grain

The chisel handle is grasped in the right hand with the thumb extended towards the blade. The cut is controlled by holding the blade firmly with the left hand, knuckles up and fingers well back from the cutting edge. The right hand is used to force the chisel into the wood, while the left hand pressing downwards on the chisel blade regulates the length and depth of cut made. To make controlled cuts work with the bevel of the chisel up.

The cutting edge will tend to follow the direction of the wood fibres. This is why it is difficult to control cuts against the grain. With cross-grained wood it may be necessary to work carefully in both directions.

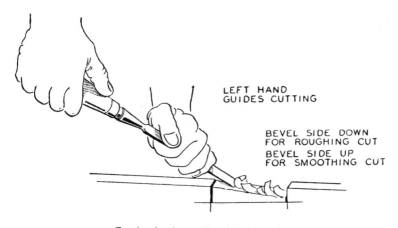

LEFT HAND
GUIDES CUTTING

BEVEL SIDE DOWN
FOR ROUGHING CUT
BEVEL SIDE UP
FOR SMOOTHING CUT

Cutting horizontally with the grain

Cutting Horizontally across the Grain

For certain types of joint it is necessary to remove waste wood from between cuts made with a saw across the grain. This calls for horizontal chiselling across the fibres of the wood.

The work should be held securely in a vice. On light work the pressure of the hand will provide sufficient driving force to the chisel. A side-to-side movement of the chisel handle while under pressure will give a shearing cut as described earlier. Remember to use a chisel small enough to enable this to be done. On heavier work, or in hardwood, a mallet can be used. Initial cuts can be made with the bevel of the chisel down. To avoid splitting at the edges, cut inwards from each side in turn towards the centre and make the cuts slightly upward so that the waste at the centre is removed last.

Finishing cuts are made with the bevel of the chisel up, using hand pressure only. With the right hand holding the handle, the blade is guided by the thumb and forefinger of the left hand which gives the chisel a sideways paring motion as it is pushed forward. Finishing cuts should also be made from each edge toward the centre. Do not cut all the way across from one edge or the far edge will be split off.

Vertical Chiselling
Vertical chiselling means cutting at right angles to the surface of the wood. Usually it involves cutting across the fibres of the

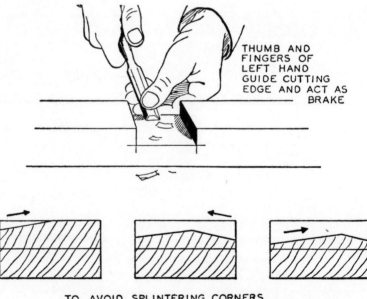

THUMB AND FINGERS OF LEFT HAND GUIDE CUTTING EDGE AND ACT AS BRAKE

TO AVOID SPLINTERING CORNERS WHEN CHISELLING ACROSS GRAIN CUT HALFWAY FROM EACH EDGE TOWARD CENTRE

Chiselling horizontally across the grain

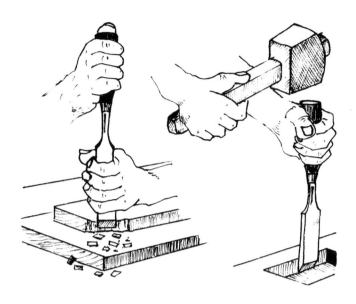

Vertical chiselling

wood as in chiselling out a mortice, for example. The work should be clamped or otherwise secured so that it cannot move under the pressure of chiselling. Work on the bench should be done with a cutting board between the workpiece and the bench, never directly on the bench top. This way there is no risk of the chisel cutting into the bench top.

When cutting across grain in hardwood, it will be necessary to drive the chisel with a mallet. Light cuts in softwood and all finishing cuts should be done by hand pressure only. Care should be taken, especially when using the mallet, to avoid splitting the wood. Be especially careful with vertical cuts with the grain—it is easy to cause splitting with these cuts. Always begin by making the necessary cuts across the grain before making cuts with the grain. The cross cuts will help check any splits which may start.

When using the mallet and chisel, grasp the chisel with the left hand as if holding a dagger for stabbing. Strike the chisel with the mallet held in the right hand. For vertical paring, again hold the chisel as if for stabbing but this time in the right hand and with the thumb pressing down on the top of

67

the handle. (Do *not* do this when using the mallet!) Use the left hand now to guide the blade and give additional driving force if needed. The cutting edge of the chisel should make a shearing cut and the shavings kept fine.

Chamfering with a Chisel

A chamfer is made by flattening the sharp corner between two surfaces at right angles to each other. A plain chamfer runs the full length of the edge and is usually made with a plane. A stopped chamfer does not run the full length. If a stopped chamfer is long enough, part of it can be planed and the ends finished with a chisel. A short, stopped chamfer must be made entirely with a chisel. A chamfer is usually made at 45°. Guide lines should be made with a pencil and *not* with a marking gauge or knife.

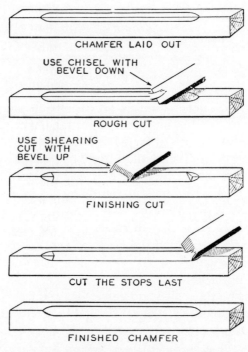

Cutting a stopped chamfer with a chisel

To cut a stopped chamfer, hold the chisel with the edge parallel to the intended slope of the chamfer and cut with the grain as in ordinary horizontal paring. Begin chiselling at one end and work toward the far end. Then turn the work round and work from the end again. Do this with care as it will mean working against the grain.

The ends of a chamfer may be either flat or curved. If flat, use the chisel with the bevel up. If curved, use with the bevel down. Unless the grain of the wood is quite straight, there is always the danger of splitting off too much wood if deep cuts are made. Rather than risk spoiling the work it is best to use light cuts throughout, even if this does take more time to remove the surplus wood. The experienced craftsman can usually safely remove most of the surplus with rough cuts and then finish off with light paring cuts.

Cutting Diagonally across the Grain
To cut a straight slanting corner, as shown in the illustration, as much waste wood as possible is first removed with a saw. The work is then gripped in a vice so that the guide line for cutting is horizontal and the chisel used as in horizontal

BEVEL DOWN
FOR ROUGHING
BEVEL UP
FOR SMOOTHING

Cutting a straight slanting corner diagonally across the grain

69

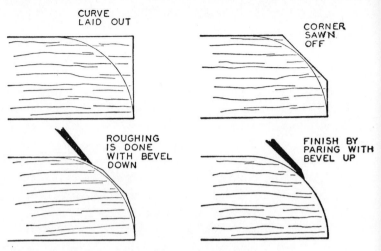

Chiselling a round corner

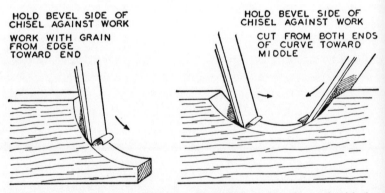

Chiselling concave curves. Hold the chisel blade against the work with the left hand. Drive the chisel with pressure from the right hand on the handle

chiselling again. To chisel a convex curve or round corner first mark out the curve, then remove as much waste as possible with a saw. Use a chisel with its bevel down to make a series of straight cuts tangent to the curve. The curve is finished by paring with the bevelled side of the chisel up. To make a concave curve the chisel is held with its bevelled side to the wood throughout the work. This stops the chisel digging into the curve too deeply. In making all these cuts, the chisel is moved sideways across the work at the same time that it is moved forward to give the required shearing cut.

Chiselling Practice

As an exercise for gaining free skill in the use of chisels there is nothing better than making a few lap joints. The simple half lap or middle lap joint is a good starting point. This is also good sawing practice. Good quality softwood is the best material to use in the beginning. When a good job can be made in softwood, the beginner should go on to test his skill on hardwood.

The first operation is to mark out the joint using a sharp knife to score through the fibres of the wood. Then, cut a shallow groove on the waste side of the knife cuts which are the guide lines for the shoulders of the joint. The grooves should be cut with a chisel, bevel side up. The shoulders of the joint are cut down almost to the horizontal guide lines

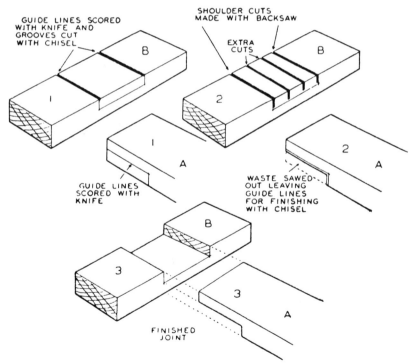

Making a half lap joint is good chiselling practice

71

with a back saw. The saw is started in the grooves which help to position the saw blade. A few extra saw cuts made between the shoulder cuts may be made to make the chiselling out of the waste easier.

The waste wood is cut away with a chisel, working inwards from both sides alternately to avoid splitting the edges. Make each cut slightly upward until down to the horizontal guide line, then carefully remove the waste remaining at the centre. Finish by paring with a very sharp chisel. Hold it flat to the wood, bevel up and make very light cuts.

When both parts of the joint are pared down to the guide lines, they are fitted together. Further paring may be necessary to obtain a good fit. The two parts should fit together firmly and snugly—it should not be necessary to force them together. Remember, practice makes perfect.

Gouges

A gouge is a chisel with a concave blade which gives it a curved cutting edge. There are two main types: one has its

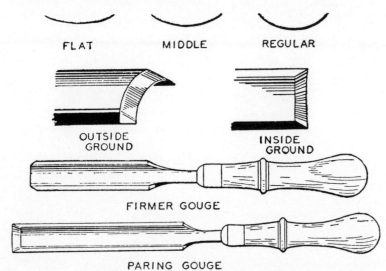

Gouges are chisels with curved cutting edges

cutting bevel ground on the inside and is known as an inside or in-cannel gouge, the other is ground on the outside and is known as outside or out-cannel gouge. The former is also known as a firmer gouge, the latter as a scribing gouge, or both may be referred to as inside or outside firmer gouges. Gouges with long, light blades are known as paring gouges and these always have an inside bevel. A version with a cranked or bent shank is available. This lifts the hand clear of the work when cutting long grooves. Three different blade curvatures are available, which are known as a flat, a middle and a regular sweep.

Gouges are used for cutting hollows and grooves and for paring shaped edges. A gouge with an inside bevel is used in the same way as a chisel with the bevel up. A gouge with an outside bevel behaves like a chisel with the bevel down and is used in the same way. A gouge is always started at the edge of a cut and driven towards the centre. This minimises splitting. To keep each cut under control, cut across the grain whenever possible.

Woodcarving

The decorative carving of wood is one of the great arts. Some men devote a lifetime to it, and it is too large a subject to more than mention in this book. When roughing out large work, the woodcarver sometimes uses the chisels and gouges of the carpenter but for the actual carved work he has special tools called carving tools. These are chisels and gouges which differ from the ordinary in that they have shaped blades which enables them to be used for a wide range of special cuts. A busy woodcarver may have fifty or sixty carving tools in regular use, his own particular choice from a range of over one thousand different types and sizes currently available.

The cutting edges of carving chisels may be square or left or right oblique (these are known as skew chisels). The blades of carving gouges are made with eleven different diameter curves or sweeps, and both gouges and chisels are available in sizes from $\frac{1}{16}$in (3mm) to about $1\frac{1}{2}$in (38mm). There are 'V'-shaped gouges called parting tools and deep, narrow 'U'-shaped gouges known as veiners. All are available with straight or bent blades, and there are also back bent and spoon bit types. Some tools flare outward to the cutting edge and are known as fishtails.

The handles of carving tools vary greatly and are made to fit nicely into the palm of the hand. They may also be struck lightly with a wooden mallet. Special carvers' mallets have round heads.

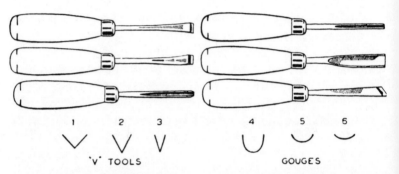

Some typical carving tools. These are chisels and gouges made especially for carving low relief designs, small models etc. Their edges are ground at the factory, but should be whetted on a fine oilstone before being used

The average craftsman who wishes to carve small objects needs only a small assortment of carving tools. The most useful are illustrated. A keen, razor-like edge should be maintained on all carving tools if they are to do their job properly.

Rasps and Files

The use of rasps and files for woodworking has long been frowned upon by craftsmen woodworkers. Their use is justified in certain instances, however. For example, in situations where it is impracticable or impossible to use a cutting tool, a file or rasp can be quite useful. They also have

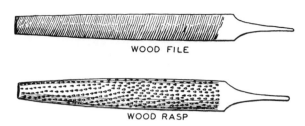

WOOD FILE

WOOD RASP

Files and rasps for woodworking

their uses for shaping, although a cutting tool gives a better finish and is more satisfying to use.

Wood rasps cut faster but leave a much rougher surface than files. The standard wood rasp is usually known as a cabinet rasp. Wood files have coarse or medium coarse, single or double cut teeth.

Surform tools, described briefly elsewhere, fit into this category of tool.

Wooden mallets. On the left a joiner's mallet and on the right, a carver's mallet

Mallets

Wooden mallets are used mainly to drive wood chisels, gouges and carving tools. They also have other uses in the workshop, for example, when assembling jointed work.

75

Generally speaking, they are used where a metal hammer would damage the tool or the work being struck.

The common joiner's mallet has a rectangular section head, is usually made of beech and comes in sizes from 4in (102mm) to 7in (178mm). This is the measurement across the side of the head. The round-headed mallet or carver's mallet is made in a variety of woods including beech. The best have heads of lignum vitae.

5
Hammers and Nails

There are several different types of hammer, some made for special purposes, others for more general use. Each different type is usually available in a range of sizes normally determined by the weight of the head in ounces. Wood-workers' hammers are used principally to drive nails, wedges and dowels, and the two most useful for these purposes are the claw hammer and the cross peen (or pein) hammer.

Claw Hammers
The claw hammer not only drives nails, it also pulls them out. It takes its name from the curved, split claw which is used to pull out nails or to rip wooden boards apart. If the claw has a pronounced curve, the hammer was designed to be more efficient at pulling nails. If the claw is only slightly curved, the hammer is better adapted to ripping than nail pulling.

A claw hammer is often part of the tool kit of every household where it is used not only to drive and pull nails but also often serves a great variety of other purposes from cracking nuts to committing murder. A good craftsman, however, does not put his hammer to such diversified uses. He does not use it to break firewood or drive cold chisels with it. He chops firewood with an axe and drives cold chisels with an engineer's hammer or something similar.

Claw hammers are available in four sizes:

Size	Weight
No 1	13oz (365g)
2	16oz (450g)
3	20oz (560g)
4	24oz (672g)

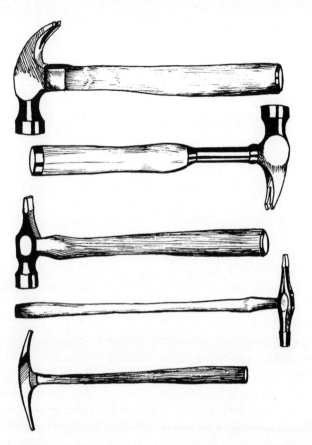

Types of hammer. From the top: a claw hammer; a ripping hammer; a cross peen (or pein) hammer; a pin hammer; an upholsterer's hammer

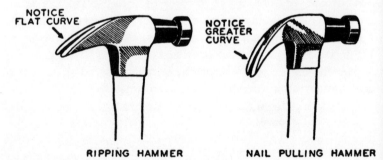

A ripping hammer and a nail-pulling hammer. The flat curvature of its claws makes the ripping hammer more efficient for pulling apart woodwork than for drawing out nails

Cross Peen Hammers

The cross peen (or pein) hammer has a head with a flat, tapered end instead of a claw. This can be used to start small nails held between the fingers before using the face to drive the nail home. Six different sizes are obtainable:

Size	Weight
No 00	6oz (168g)
0	8oz (225g)
1	10oz (280g)
2	12oz (336g)
3	14oz (392g)
4	16oz (450g)

A lightweight hammer with the same shape head is known as a pin hammer. This has a longer and much thinner handle than the standard hammer and has a head weight of only about $3\frac{1}{2}$oz (98g). It is useful for driving small nails such as panel pins etc.

Specifications of a Good Hammer

The cheap hammer has a cast-iron head, whose face is not always accurately ground. It soon chips and loses its shape. It slips off the heads of nails and is an ideal tool for driving nails crooked and hurting fingers.

The head of a first-class hammer is not cast. It is drop forged from tough alloy steel and is heat treated and tempered so that it is twice as strong as ordinary steel. A cast head is made by pouring white hot steel into a sand mould. A drop-forged head is made by hammering red-hot metal into a steel die. A cast head is therefore brittle; a drop-forged head is really tough although it too can chip if misused.

The head of a good hammer is accurately ground to shape. The face is usually ground smooth—or it may be slightly domed—and the edge is given a slight bevel to minimise chipping.

The handle is normally made from rough, seasoned, straight-grained hickory or ash shaped to fit the hand at one end and tapered towards the head to give the hammer its 'spring'. An important quality of a good hammer handle is its spring which gives the user better control of the tool and eases the strain on his muscles. That end of the handle which is fitted into the hammer head is expanded into the tapered eye of the head by wooden and metal wedges so that it cannot come off easily. The claw hammer, which has to withstand the force of levering when used to pull nails, has an especially deep, rectangular eye. Known as an adze eye, this provides a better gripping surface for the wedged handle. Modern steel or fibreglass shafted hammers have head and handle permanently fitted together. These handles have rubber, plastic or leather sleeves to provide a comfortable grip.

Hammer Sizes
The lighter hammers are used for driving small nails, the heaviest for driving large nails into soft wood or medium-sized nails into hard wood. When the hammer used is too light for the job it will cause a nail to bend. It should be so heavy that a large nail can be driven in completely with five or six blows. A 16oz (450g) claw hammer and an 8oz (225g) cross peen are good choices for general use.

New Handles for Hammers
When a hammer handle breaks or becomes too loose, a new one is easily fitted. Well-seasoned hickory or ash make the best handles. These can be made or bought from tool dealers. The portion of a broken handle which may remain in a hammer head may be difficult to remove because of the wedges which hold it in place. Drilling away the wood around the wedges and then splitting out what remains will usually solve this problem.

It may be necessary to reduce the end of a new handle before it will go into the head. This can be done with a chisel, knife or rasp. But remember the handle must fit very tightly into the head. The small end of the handle goes into the head, and the opposite end is struck sharply against the bench top or other solid surface until the handle is in place and flush with

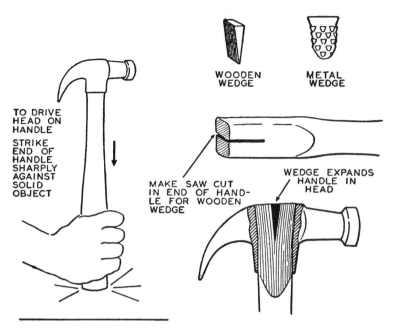

WOODEN WEDGE

METAL WEDGE

TO DRIVE HEAD ON HANDLE

STRIKE END OF HANDLE SHARPLY AGAINST SOLID OBJECT

MAKE SAW CUT IN END OF HAND- LE FOR WOODEN WEDGE

WEDGE EXPANDS HANDLE IN HEAD

Fitting a hammer with a new handle

the top of the hammer head. The wedges are then driven in to expand the handle in the eye. When a wooden wedge is used a slot must first be sawn in the end of the handle.

If a hammer head works loose it may sometimes be tightened up by immersing in water. This is, however, only a temporary measure. A hammer with a loose head is a very dangerous tool.

How to Use a Hammer
Using a hammer to drive nails seems too easy to require explanation. But a great many people who own hammers and think they know how to do the job should read on if they want to avoid bruised fingers, bent nails and damaged work. First, choose the right nail for the job (see later in this chapter) and a hammer which suits the nail. Grasp the hammer handle firmly with the end practically flush with the lower edge of the palm. Do not hold it close to the head and 'choke' it. Hold the nail near its point with thumb and forefinger of the opposite

81

hand and place the point at the exact spot where it is to be driven in. Unless the nail is to be purposely driven in at an angle, it should be held perpendicular to the surface of the work. Rest the face of the hammer at its centre on the head of the nail, raise the hammer slightly and give the nail one or two light taps to start the nail and fix your aim. Then get your fingers out of the way and drive the nail in as far as you want it to go, hitting the nail square on its head each time.

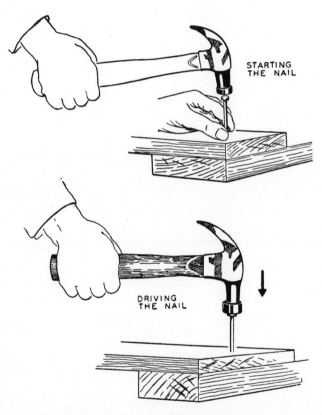

The right way to drive a nail. Grasp the nail near its point with thumb and forefinger. Place the point on the work and strike the head with one or two light blows of the hammer to start the point into the wood. Then get your fingers out of the way and drive the nail in with firm blows. At the instant when the hammer strikes the nail, the direction of its motion should be parallel to the axis of the nail

The wrist and arm motion used depends upon the power of the blows required. Small nails require light blows, which are struck almost entirely with a wrist movement. Slightly heavier or medium blows need both wrist and forearm motion while the heavy blows needed to drive a large nail come from wrist, forearm and shoulder. Do not attack a nail viciously. On the other hand, do not be too timid. Nails are properly driven with a few, positive, firm blows and not with either a pile-driving whack or a series of light taps. Always strike a nail squarely with the centre of the hammer face. Do not strike with the side or cheek of the hammer head. Dirt, rust or grease on the hammer face will cause it to slip on the nail; therefore keep the face clean.

When a nail is going in straight, proceed as above. If it starts to go crooked, striking the nail with the hammer face at a slight angle will force the nail forwards, backwards or sideways depending on the angle. This is the trick used to straighten up a nail not going in the right direction.

If a nail bends when it is being driven in, take it out and throw it away. Start another in its place. If the second nail also bends, investigation is called for. If the nail appears to be striking a knot or a hidden nail or other obstruction, it will be necessary to take the nail out again. Try driving a new nail in a new place. If the wood is exceptionally hard at that point then it may be necessary to drill a small hole to overcome the problem.

Nailing

Whenever possible nails should be driven in across grain; their holding power is much reduced when driven into end grain. Never put nails close together in a straight line. This will cause the wood to split. For the same reason avoid nailing near an edge. Instead, you should 'stagger' the nails. If splitting is a real problem, try using thinner or oval nails, or drill holes smaller in diameter than the nails to be used partly through the wood to be joined. Always fix a thin board to a thick one and not vice versa. If you must nail into end grain, drive nails obliquely for improved holding power. To fasten the end of one piece of wood to another it may be necessary to employ a method known as toenailing or skewnailing. Start the first nail straight, then tip it up at a suitable angle and drive it part way home. Start the second nail at the opposite side, then drive both nails alternately. This corrects any tendency for the vertical piece of wood to move position under the hammer blows.

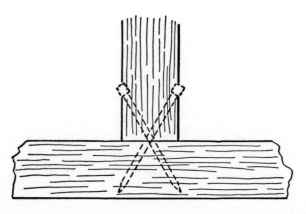

Toe nailing. It may be necessary to drive nails obliquely in order to fasten the end of one piece of wood to the side of another.

For extra security in some instances nails may be clinched or clenched. For this, nails long enough to go right through the pieces of wood being joined must be used. Each nail is driven through and the work turned over. The protruding points are then bent over and hammered down into the fibres of the wood. The work should rest on a solid surface for this. If the job is a fixture a second hammer can be held to the head of the nail while its point is clinched over.

When nailing tongue and groove floor-boarding, nails may be concealed by being carefully driven through the back of the tongue at an angle of about 50°. This also draws each board closer to the last one.

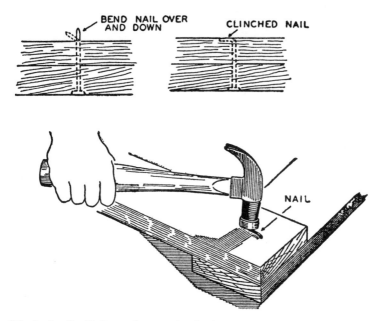

BEND NAIL OVER AND DOWN

CLINCHED NAIL

NAIL

Clinched nails. Nails are frequently clinched to give them greater holding power. The nail must be long enough to completely penetrate the wood so that the point protrudes. The point is then bent over in line with the grain of the wood and hammered down between the wood fibres. If bent across the grain, the point is hammered down until it crushes the fibres. Clinching must be done with care to avoid splitting the wood. The work should rest on a solid surface.

Concealing a Nail

In work where the nail head must not show or must be inconspicuous, it is driven well below the surface. The hole in the wood over the nail head is then filled in and made flush with the surface. Oval-headed nails or panel pins (described later) are used for this, and a tool called a nail set is used to 'set' them below the surface. Nail sets are made in three or four different sizes usually from $\frac{1}{32}$in (1mm) to about $\frac{1}{8}$in (3mm), the size indicated being the diameter of the small end of the tapered shank. The end of a good nail set should be hollowed or cupped—this prevents it from 'walking' or slipping off the nail head.

Use a nail set of a size which will not enlarge the hole made by the head of the nail. Hold the tool between thumb and

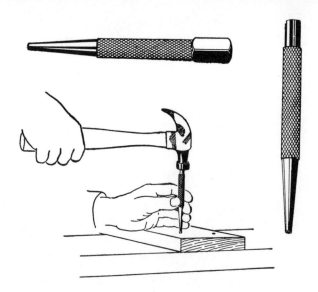

A nail set is used to drive the head of a finishing nail below the surface of the work

forefinger, and press the small end firmly against the head of the nail. Rest the little finger on the work to steady your hand and help keep the nail set from slipping. Then, using a suitable hammer, drive the nail head below the surface with a light tap. The resulting hole can be filled with either a small wooden plug, with wood filler or with a mixture of sawdust and glue. When dry the surface is sanded flat.

How to Draw a Nail

In order to pull out a nail with a claw hammer, it is necessary for the head of the nail to be far enough above the surface of the work so that the claws of the hammer can be slipped underneath. The slot between the claws should go well round the nail and under the nail head. Then raise the hammer handle until it is nearly vertical. If the nail is a short one, this will withdraw it completely from the work. If the nail is long and the hammer handle is pulled past the vertical position, the nail will begin to bend. This will serve only to cause the nail hole to enlarge and mar the surface of the work. Moreover, when the hammer handle passes the vertical position, most of the effective leverage is lost and a great deal of force is required to draw the nail any further.

The simple remedy is to slip a block of waste wood between the hammer head and the work surface so that the handle is again nearly horizontal and the leverage increased. This will also apply the pulling force of the claws in the proper direction so that the nail is drawn out without enlarging the hole already made by the nail. When long nails, only partially driven into the wood, must be pulled out, it may be necessary to start the pulling operation with a block of wood under the hammer head in order to get the correct leverage to begin with. Another method of withdrawing nails is to use a wrecking or ripping bar. This is a sort of curved crowbar

How to draw out a nail

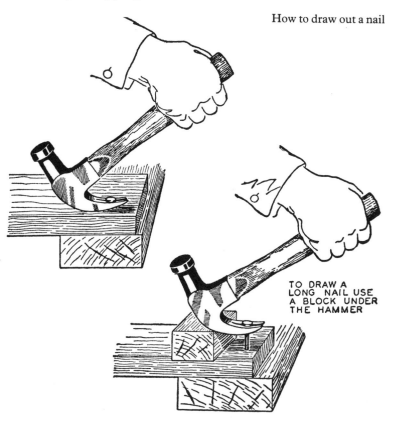

TO DRAW A
LONG NAIL USE
A BLOCK UNDER
THE HAMMER

made from drop-forged hexagon tool steel. The curved end has a claw end like the claw hammer. The straight end usually has a chisel edge. It is ofen used for opening packing cases.

About Nails

In the dictionary a nail is defined as 'a fastening device for wood made from round or oval wire, having a point at one end and a head at the other'. But nails are much more significant than the dictionary's definition of them. Nails are a quick and easy means of fastening pieces of wood together or of fixing things on to wood. They are made in a wide variety of types and a large number of different sizes. Each has a particular quality which makes it the best to use for certain jobs. Their main advantages lie in their relative cheapness and the ease with which they can be used. Joints held by nails alone, however, have limited strength and there is the added problem of split wood when nails are being driven in.

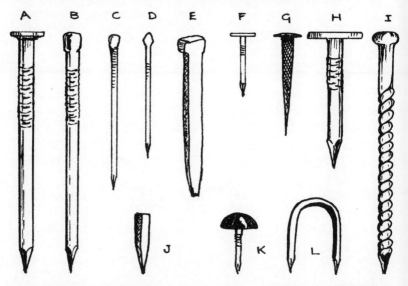

Representative types of nail: A round common wire nail; B oval common wire nail; C panel pin; D hardboard pin; E cut nail; F escutcheon pin; G cut tack; H roofing nail; I screw nail; J sprig; K upholstery pin; L staple

Nails have been developed from the simple wooden peg of ancient craftsmen. One hundred years ago they were hammered into shape by hand from wrought iron, then they were cut by simple machines from iron sheet. Today nails are produced by automatic machines from mild steel wire and in various other metals, copper, brass, and other alloys in hundreds of different shapes and sizes.

The simple form of the ordinary nail has been modified to meet many specialised requirements. Changing the general proportions and the size or shape of the head, shank and point produces special nails for all sorts of uses. The names used to describe these different nails may vary from place to place. The illustrations will help sort out any confusion. Sold usually by weight, nails are designated by type and length. In America many nails are sized by the penny system. Originally this system indicated price per hundred; today it relates to the length of the nail.

Common Nails
These come in two main types for general use. Both are known as wire nails or common wire nails but one type is round in section while the other is oval. Usually the top part of the shank is serrated to give a better grip in the fibres of the wood. They are available in sizes from about 1in (25mm) up to 6in (150mm) in ½in steps. Round nails have flat, round heads. They are general purpose nails used for timber framing, fencing, crates etc and in all rough carpentry where it does not matter if the head shows. Oval nails, sometimes known as finishing nails, have oval or 'brad' heads. Their shape makes them less likely to split the wood when they are being driven in and their small heads can be punched out of sight below the surface of the work. They should be driven in so that they are in line with the grain of the wood.

Panel Pins
A third commonly used nail is the fine, light-weight nail known as the panel pin. It is used mainly to secure plywood

and hardboard panels, when fixing mouldings etc, and in fine cabinet work. It is a thin wire nail and its very small tapered head is easily punched below the work surface. They range in size from $\frac{1}{2}$in (12mm) to 2in (50mm). Hardboard nails or pins are similar to panel pins but are made in a harder steel, and are more suitable for driving into this particular material, which tends to bend ordinary panel pins.

Cut Nails
A nail which resembles the old handmade nail is the cut nail. Stamped out from mild steel sheet these nails are sharply rectangular in section and have good holding qualities. They are used mainly in building work, for holding floorboards etc.

Escutcheon Pins
Several types of small nails, pins, brads, tacks etc are made for special purposes. One of these is a short brass, or brassed, nail used for fixing small metal fittings to wood. These are known as escutcheon pins.

Upholstery Nails
For fixing fabrics such as upholstery or carpet material, a number of different types of nail can be used. These include cut tacks, which are made in black or blued mild steel. Sharply pointed, these are sometimes called thumb tacks on account of the ease with which they may be started by a press of the thumb then driven home with a hammer. Tacks come in sizes from $\frac{1}{2}$in (12mm) to 1in (25mm). A lot of upholstery is now held not with nails but with wire staples. Fired into the work by means of a hand gun, this method is used because it is quicker than hammering in nails. Brass chair nails, also called upholstery pins, have large domed decorative heads and are used for fixing fabrics where nailing or stapling would be visible and unsightly.

Sprigs
These are short, cut tacks without heads and their main use is in holding glass in place in window frames.

Roofing Nails
For fixing roofing felt and other similar sheet material, special nails known as clout nails are used. These have large flat heads and are available from ¾in (19mm) to 2in (50mm) in length. Because of their use outdoors, they are galvanised against rusting. Many other types of nails are galvanised for outdoor use.

Copper Nails
For boat building, nails made from copper or bronze are used as a safeguard against corrosion.

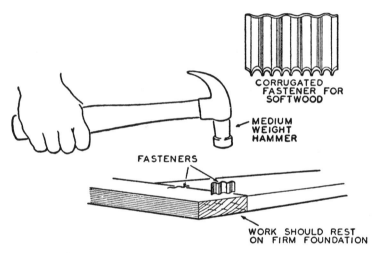

Corrugated fasteners or wiggle nails are used to fasten wood surfaces side by side

Corrugated Fasteners
Sometimes descriptively called 'Wiggle Nails', these are special nails used in rough constructional work, packing cases etc. They consist of a short length of thin corrugated steel strip with one of its edges sharpened. They are driven in across two adjacent boards by a series of light hammer blows evenly distributed along their outside edge.

91

Staples
Wire staples are 'U'-shaped nails used to fix netting, wire fencing etc. Usually they are galvanised for outdoor use.

Screw Nails
Improved forms of several nail types are available now for use particularly with new types of sheet building material. These have threaded shanks and are sometimes known as screw nails. The threads grip the wood fibres and give improved holding qualities.

6

Screws and Screwdrivers

Wood screws have much greater holding power than nails. They pull the two parts of the work together more tightly and when properly driven they are neater in appearance than nails. A further advantage is that work held together by screws is easily taken apart and put together again without damage. Their disadvantages are that they are more expensive than nails and they take longer to fix.

Types of Wood Screws

The common wood screws are made from mild steel and of brass. They have countersunk heads (flat head), round heads or raised (oval) heads. Steel screws generally have a bright steel finish but, as this rusts easily, they are obtainable plated in chrome, nickel, brass, cadmium or galvanised with zinc. 'Antique' finishes in copper or bronze are also available. Black-japanned, round-head screws are steel screws dip-treated in black enamel. Solid brass screws do not rust, but they cost much more than steel screws and, being of a softer metal, they are not equal in strength. Brass screws are used in situations where their non-rusting qualities are important, with brass fitting and in high class work of all kinds. Brass screws should always be used in oak; the tannic acid in this wood corrodes steel.

Wood Screw Sizes
Wood screws are sized according to their diameter and their length. The length is indicated in inches or fractions thereof. The diameter is indicated by a number—the gauge number.

93

The smallest diameter is no 0 and the largest common size is no 14. Standards for screw sizes have been established so that gauge numbers of different manufactures are, within accepted tolerances, all alike.

The diameter or gauge of all woodscrews is measured across the shank as indicated in the illustration by A. The length measurement of countersunk-head screws is the overall length of the screw. Round-head screws are measured from their point to the underside of the head; raised-head screws from their point to the edge of the head. The following table shows the standard diameter of wood screws indicated by the numbers 1 to 14.

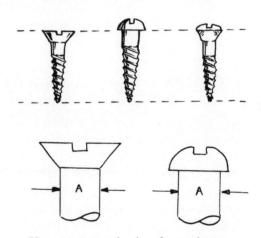

How to measure the size of a wood screw

The Diameter of Standard Wood Screws

Gauge Number	Basic	Diameter Maximum	Minimum
1	·073	·077	·066
2	·086	·090	·079
3	·099	·103	·092
4	·112	·116	·105
5	·125	·129	·118
6	·138	·142	·131
7	·151	·155	·144

The Diameter of Standard Wood Screws

Gauge Number	Basic	Diameter Maximum	Minimum
8	·164	·168	·157
9	·177	·181	·170
10	·190	·194	·183
11	·203	·207	·196
12	·216	·220	·209
14	·242	·246	·235

Wood screws. These full-size sketches may be used to identify wood screws Nos 1–14

Special Screws

Several types of screw are produced for special and specific purposes. Some of these are described here.

Chipboard Screws

Ordinary wood screws have a single spiral thread running from the point to about two-thirds the length of the screw. Screws with twin paralleled threads often running right up to the screw head are also made. These are not only quicker to drive in but also give added hold, ie they grip into the work better. For this last reason they are best used when working with manmade composite boards, such as chipboard, which hold conventional screws poorly.

Philips and Pozidriv Screws

The heads of all common screws are slotted to take the blade of a conventional screwdriver. The slot is a simple cut across the head of the screw. Philips and Pozidriv screws have instead a cross slot in the centre of the head designed so that there is less tendency for the screwdriver to slip out when the screw is being driven or removed. Special screwdrivers are required for use with these screws (see later in this chapter).

95

Special screws: A chipboard screw; B Philips screw head; C Pozidriv screw head; D dome-capped mirror screw

Mirror Screws

These are steel countersunk-head screws which have a threaded hole in the centre of the head to accept a decorative, screw-in domed cover. This cover may be chromed or brass and its purpose is to cover the screw head when fixing panels, mirrors etc.

Screwed Hooks and Eyes

Although these are not true screws—they have no screw-driver slot—they are threaded in the same way as conventional screws. Available in bright steel, plated steel and brass, they come in a range of sizes and types to suit a variety of purposes. When fixing them in hardwood, a pilot hole should first be drilled. For fixing the smaller sizes in soft wood, a bradawl will suffice.

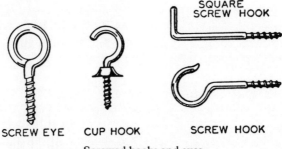

SCREW EYE   CUP HOOK   SCREW HOOK

Screwed hooks and eyes

Screw Sockets and Cups

Frequently confused, these are both used with countersunk screws for neatness of appearance and in situations where the screws may need to be removed and replaced from time to time. The screw socket is recessed flush with the surface after countersinking the wood, while the screw cup is a raised collar which lies on the surface of the wood. It is used mainly when fixing materials, panels etc too thin for countersinking.

Lag Screws
These have square heads and no screwdriver slot, and resemble machine bolts. They are driven into place and withdrawn with a spanner and not a screwdriver. They are used mainly in heavy construction work and also to fasten machinery and heavy metal parts to beams and wooden floors etc. A pilot hole and a clearance hole must always be bored for a lag screw. A metal washer should be used under the head so that the head is not pulled into the wood when the screw is tightened.

Lag screws are sized according to diameter and length. Common diameters are $\frac{1}{4}$in (6mm), $\frac{5}{16}$in (7·5mm), $\frac{3}{8}$in (9mm), $\frac{7}{16}$in (10·5mm), $\frac{1}{2}$in (12mm) and $\frac{5}{8}$in (16mm). Common lengths range from 2in (50mm) to 6in (152mm) in $\frac{1}{2}$in (12mm) steps, and from 6in (152mm) to 12in (305mm) in 1in (25mm) steps. They are normally made in black iron or they may be galvanised.

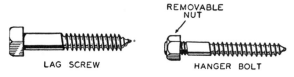

Screws for heavy construction

Hanger Bolts
The head of a hanger bolt is a loose hexagonal nut which can be removed with a spanner. Hanger bolts are used to fasten machinery etc to a wooden foundation. If a lag screw is driven in and out of the same hole several times, it loses some of its holding power. In order to remove a machine fastened with hanger bolts it is not necessary to withdraw the whole bolt.

Only the nut which forms the head is unscrewed, thus keeping the thread in the wood intact.

Screwdrivers

A screwdriver is used for tightening or loosening slotted screws. It is a tool which is often abused, for it is difficult to convince some that a screwdriver is not a handy combination tool for use as a small crowbar, chisel or can-opener as well as for driving screws. Misusing a screwdriver often spoils it for its intended purpose.

Most screwdrivers are somewhat alike in general appearance, but their shapes and sizes vary in design and construction according to the work for which they are intended. For example, opticians' and watchmakers' screwdrivers, which are used for fine precision work, are small in size and are turned with the tips of the thumb and forefingers. But for heavy engineering work there are square shanked screwdrivers made in very rugged sizes and often turned with the aid of a spanner in order to apply extra force.

Types of Screwdriver

The traditional screwdriver for woodworking is the type known as the cabinet screwdriver. This has a handle which is oval and bulbous to fill the palm of the hand. This shape gives a very positive grip. Handles were once always of boxwood or beech but now plastic or occasionally a hardwood of some kind are used. The cylindrical blade may have a flared tip or be ground back to give a slightly tapered end. Wooden handles are strengthened with a metal ferrule but plastic handles are moulded directly on to the blade.

Screwdrivers with straight, fluted handles are also used, although these are often described as engineers' screwdrivers. These handles may be in coloured plastic or hardwood. In some the blade extends right through the handle, making them very strong. The fluting of the handle is intended to provide a good gripping surface but in fact the bulbous

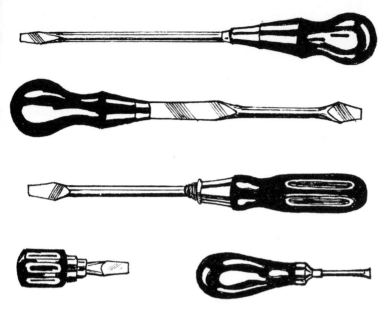

Four screwdrivers and a bradawl

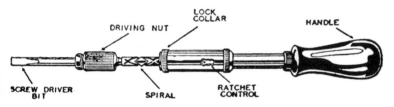

LOCK COLLAR

DRIVING NUT

HANDLE

SCREW DRIVER BIT

SPIRAL

RATCHET CONTROL

Automatic screwdriver. Pushing the handle turns the blade. It can be used both to drive and to withdraw screws. The mechanism can be locked so that the tool can be used as an ordinary screwdriver

Phillips screwdriver

handle of the cabinet screwdriver, although smooth, works equally well, if not better. The cylindrical blade of these screwdrivers is usually flattened and ground to a taper end.

Those screwdrivers known as rachet screwdrivers allow the user to drive or slacken screws without a change of grip.

This facility is useful in awkward places and for repetition work. The rachet, which can be set to work clockwise or anticlockwise, or taken out of use altogether, enables the handle to 'freewheel' on the blade if and when required. A screwdriver known as a spiral rachet or 'Yankee' screwdriver combines this rachet drive with a pump action, turning screws by pressure only. This is a useful tool for production work involving the use of a lot of screws.

The special screwdrivers used with Philips and Pozidriv screws have cylindrical blades. The pointed tip of the Philips blade is ground with four flutes to form the required cross end. The Pozidriv tip is similar but has a square point.

Combination Screwdrivers

These are basically a handle into which can be fitted different sizes and types of screwdriver blade. Frequently the blades are stored inside the handle, which is hollow for this purpose.

Screwdriver Bits

Large screws can be driven and removed more easily with a screwdriver bit fitted into a brace than with an ordinary screwdriver. The brace provides more leverage. A screwdriver bit is a robust screwdriver blade with a square shank made to fit in the chuck of a carpenter's brace. Bits are made in several widths up to about $\frac{3}{4}$in (19mm). The bit chosen should fit the slot of the screw snugly and should be the same width as the head of the screw.

Screwdriver Sizes

Screwdrivers are made in many different sizes. A good craftsman always has several sizes ready for use. At least two or three sizes should be in every tool kit. The size of a screwdriver is indicated by the length of the blade and excludes the length of the handle. A 4in (101mm) screwdriver has a blade 4in (101mm) long, for example. The width of the blade at the tip also varies. A blade with a narrow tip is

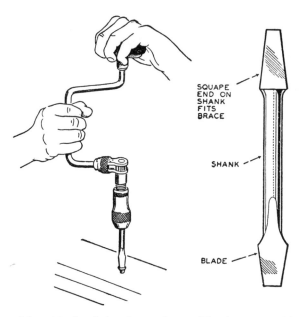

SQUARE
END ON
SHANK
FITS
BRACE

SHANK

BLADE

A screwdriver bit for fitting into a brace. The brace provides greater leverage than an ordinary screwdriver and requires less effort to drive

intended for small screws; one with a large tip for larger screws. There is no 'all-purpose' screwdriver. The screwdriver must fit the job.

Too much emphasis cannot be placed upon the fact that the tip of the screwdriver blade should fit the slot in the screw. The thickness of the blade must fit snugly into the screw slot and the width of the blade should be close to the length of the slot. If it is too wide, the tip of the blade may mark the work around the screw head and leave a ragged finish. If too narrow and not thick enough, the tip of the blade will twist and burr the edge of the screw slot. It may also damage the screwdriver tip. A blade which fits well in the slot is easier to keep in place when turning a screw than one which does not.

More power can be applied with less effort with a long screwdriver than with a short one. There is also less risk of it slipping out of the slot. Of course, limited space sometimes prevents the use of a long screwdriver. Very short screwdrivers called 'stubbies' are made for use in confined spaces.

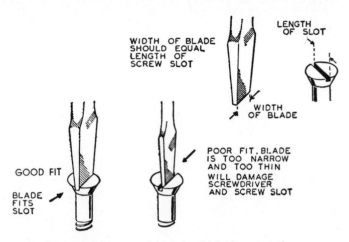

WIDTH OF BLADE
SHOULD EQUAL
LENGTH OF
SCREW SLOT

LENGTH OF SLOT

WIDTH OF BLADE

GOOD FIT

BLADE FITS SLOT

POOR FIT. BLADE IS TOO NARROW AND TOO THIN
WILL DAMAGE SCREWDRIVER AND SCREW SLOT

The tip of the screwdriver should fit the screw slot

While it may be true that a cheap screwdriver is better than none at all, it really pays to buy a good one. The handle and especially the quality of the steel in the blade are much superior to the equivalent parts in a cheap tool. So too is the method of fixing the two parts together. The blade of better steel will not twist or become burred as easily. Moreover the tip of a good screwdriver is ground to a better shape, more parallel in section than cheaper varieties which usually have too much taper. A blade which tapers too quickly from the tip has a tendency to rise out of the screw slot when being turned.

Driving a Screw
Use the longest screwdriver convenient for the job whose blade fits the screw slot. Centre the tip of the blade in the screw slot. Hold the screwdriver firmly in the right (or left) hand with the head of the handle against the palm and the thumb, fingers grasping the handle near the ferrule. To drive a screw *in*, turn it *clockwise*. To remove or withdraw a screw, turn it in the opposite or *anticlockwise* direction. When taking a fresh grip on the handle, steady the tip of the screwdriver and keep it pressed in the screw slot with the left (or right) hand. The fingers should grasp the blade just above the tip. Relax the grip when the screwdriver is turned.

102

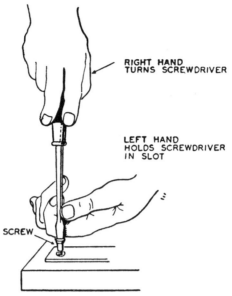

RIGHT HAND
TURNS SCREWDRIVER

LEFT HAND
HOLDS SCREWDRIVER
IN SLOT

SCREW

Use both hands to drive a screw

When driving or withdrawing a screw, keep the screwdriver aligned with the screw and keep it in the screw slot. The trick is to concentrate the main effort on applying *pressure* to the screwdriver and less on turning the screw, *not* the other way round. A little soap or candle wax rubbed into the threads of a wood screw makes it easier to drive in.

Removing a Tight Screw
When a tight screw is to be removed and it cannot be turned at the first attempt, it can often be started if it is first given a slight twist in a clockwise direction, that is, as though tightening it. This will often free the thread. Sometimes it is helpful if the screw is worked both ways. It will usually back out a little more each time this is done.

Often a really stubborn or rusted screw can be started by means of a sharp blow to the handle of the screwdriver. This is best done using a screwdriver whose blade goes right through the handle.

A tight screw cannot be removed with a screwdriver which does not fit properly in the screw slot. If it does not, then the

103

blade will ride up and the slot will be 'chewed' so that the job becomes even more difficult. A screw with a damaged slot may be impossible to remove. If you damage the slot of a screw when it is being put in, take it out and throw it away. Do not use it again. Screws with chewed slots look unsightly, and the slivers of metal which come from them are very sharp.

Boring a Hole for a Screw

If a screw is driven in without first boring a pilot hole for the threaded part, the work will be unnecessarily difficult. The wood may be split or, particularly in hardwood, the screw head may be twisted off. Holes for small screws in softwood can usually be made with a bradawl. For large screws in both softwood and hardwood, holes must be bored with a suitable twist drill. If the wood is soft, bore the hole only about half the length of the screw but, if the wood is hard, the depth of the hole should be the same as the length of the screw.

Drill Sizes for Pilot and Clearance Holes for Screws Gauge 1 to 14

Gauge of screw	SOFTWOOD				HARDWOOD			
	Pilot in	mm	Clearance in	mm	Pilot in	mm	Clearance in	mm
1	Use		Use		$\frac{3}{64}$	1·2	$\frac{5}{64}$	2
2					$\frac{1}{16}$	1·6	$\frac{3}{32}$	2·5
3					$\frac{1}{16}$	1·6	$\frac{7}{64}$	3
4	a		a		$\frac{5}{64}$	2	$\frac{1}{8}$	3·5
5					$\frac{5}{64}$	2	$\frac{1}{8}$	3.5
6	bradawl		bradawl		$\frac{5}{64}$	2	$\frac{5}{32}$	4
7	$\frac{1}{16}$	1·6	$\frac{3}{32}$	2·5	$\frac{3}{32}$	2·5	$\frac{5}{32}$	4
8	$\frac{1}{16}$	1·6	$\frac{3}{32}$	2·5	$\frac{3}{32}$	2·5	$\frac{3}{16}$	5
9	$\frac{5}{64}$	2	$\frac{5}{32}$	4	$\frac{1}{8}$	3·5	$\frac{3}{16}$	5
10	$\frac{5}{64}$	2	$\frac{5}{32}$	4	$\frac{1}{8}$	3·5	$\frac{7}{32}$	5·75
12	$\frac{5}{64}$	2	$\frac{5}{32}$	4	$\frac{1}{8}$	3·5	$\frac{1}{4}$	6·5
14	$\frac{7}{64}$	3	$\frac{7}{32}$	5.75	$\frac{5}{32}$	4	$\frac{1}{4}$	6.5

In hardwood, if the screw is particularly large or the wood especially hard, or when putting in a brass screw, it is necessary to bore a pilot hole and then to enlarge this at the top with a second drill of the same, or slightly larger, diameter as the unthreaded shank of the screw.

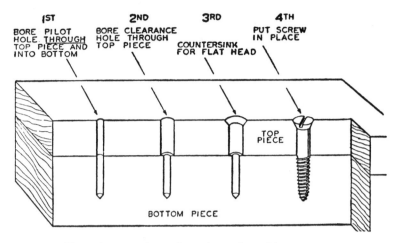

1ST	2ND	3RD	4TH
BORE PILOT HOLE THROUGH TOP PIECE AND INTO BOTTOM	BORE CLEARANCE HOLE THROUGH TOP PIECE	COUNTERSINK FOR FLAT HEAD	PUT SCREW IN PLACE

TOP PIECE

BOTTOM PIECE

Fastening two pieces of wood together with screws

When two pieces of wood are to be fastened tightly together with screws, two sets of holes must be drilled. The lower piece of wood is drilled as described above so that the screw 'bites' or 'takes hold' only in this piece. The top piece is drilled with a 'clearance' hole, that is, one slightly larger than the screw shank. In this way the top piece is clamped to the lower piece only by the pressure of the screw head.

Fastening a Metal Fitting in Place

Certain hinges, door catches etc require that the wood be recessed before they can be mounted. Locate the position of the fitting on the work and mark round it with a sharp pencil or score it with a knife blade. Using this line as a guide, cut the recess with a chisel. The procedure then is the same whether the fittings are recessed or not:

1. Position the fitting on the work and mark the screw holes.
2. Bore the pilot holes as previously described.
3. Bore clearance holes if the wood is hard or the screws are long.
4. Use screws of the largest size that will pass easily through the holes in the fitting. If the fitting is countersunk, use oval-head or countersunk-head screws which properly fit the countersink. If the holes are not countersunk, round-

105

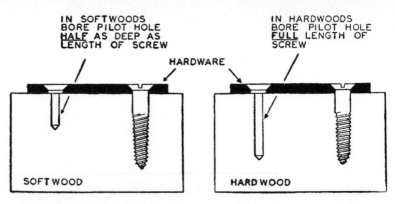

How to fasten hardware in place. The wood is shown in section so that the pilot holes and screws are revealed

head screws should be used. Countersunk-head screws should always be used in hinges where the two faces come together.

Twisting Off of a Brass Screw
Since a brass screw is not as strong as a steel screw, the head and shank can twist off more easily. This is apt to occur when a brass screw is driven into hardwood. Rubbing the screw thread on a piece of soap will help to avoid this. A more certain method is to drive in a steel screw of the same size first. The steel screw is then removed and the brass screw put in its place. The steel screw cuts a thread in the wood into which the brass screw will go easily.

How to Conceal a Screw
Screws are sometimes set below the surface of the wood and concealed with a wooden plug. Wooden plugs of various diameters can be cut with a tool called a plug cutter. This fits into and is turned with a brace or drill. Plugs should be cut from the same kind of wood as that in which they are to be inserted and the grain should match as closely as possible. They should be cut so that the grain runs across the plug and not lengthwise.

First bore a hole at least $\frac{3}{8}$in (9mm) deep with a bit the same size as the wooden plug to be used. Then bore the proper pilot and clearance holes for the screw to be used. Drive in the screw really tight and as far as it will go. Select a suitable plug, put glue on its sides, and insert it in the hole with the grain on the end of the plug running in the same direction as the grain on the surface of the wood. Press the plug in as far as it will go. When the glue has dried, use a chisel or a plane to pare the plug off level with the surface.

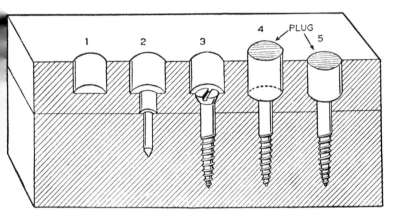

How to conceal a screw with a wooden plug. 1 Bore a hole to fit the plug. 2 Bore the pilot and clearance holes for the screw. 3 Drive the screw in place. 4 Drive in the plug, which has glue on its sides. 5 When the glue has dried, pare the top of the plug off so that it is even with the surface

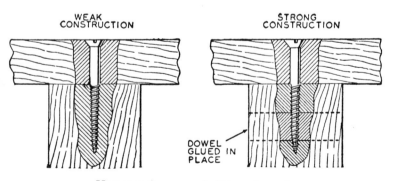

How to make a screw hold in end wood

107

Screws in End Grain

Screws do not hold well in end grain. Where the type of butt joint where screwing into end grain is used, it can be greatly strengthened by means of a dowel as illustrated. A hole is bored across the grain and into this is glued a tight-fitting dowel. The dowel is located so that screws pass through it and improve their holding power in the work.

Misusing a Screwdriver

The ordinary screwdriver will withstand considerable twisting strain but it is not intended for prying or chiselling. If used for prying lids off tins etc, it may bend and it is difficult to make it perfectly straight again. A screwdriver which is even slightly bent is difficult to keep in the slot of a screw. When a screwdriver is used as a substitute for a chisel or punch and you strike the handle with a hammer, there is a good chance that the handle will split or shatter. If you must use a screwdriver in this way, use judgement so as not to strain the tool or better still, wherever possible, keep an old screwdriver just for such purposes.

Remember that the tip of a screwdriver is hardened to prevent it becoming burred on screw heads. The tip is harder and therefore more brittle than the rest of the blade. The shank will bend but the tip will break if strained too much.

Dressing a Screwdriver Blade

Dressing a blade is a term used by craftsmen to mean putting in order or adjusting. Since a screwdriver is not a cutting tool, it does not need to be resharpened. It must, however, be dressed or kept in condition by grinding or by filing with a flat file.

If filed, the screwdriver should be held in a vice. The tip of the blade is made straight across the end, at right angles to the shank. The faces near the tip should be made parallel or almost parallel to each other. Avoid having too much taper.

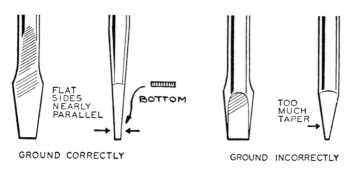

FLAT SIDES NEARLY PARALLEL

BOTTOM

TOO MUCH TAPER

GROUND CORRECTLY

GROUND INCORRECTLY

How to dress a screwdriver blade

When a screwdriver is dressed on a grindstone, aim for the same shape as described above. Remember not to hold the blade against the wheel for too long. The friction may overheat the steel and the tip will lose its temper and become soft. When a blade is being reground, dip it in water frequently to cool it. If the blade becomes too hot, it discolours; blue or yellow means the temper has been altered.

7
Adhesives and Their Use

Gluing is frequently the most satisfactory method of fastening wood together. It is used almost to the exclusion of nails and screws in fine cabinet, furniture and pattern making. Glued joints between side and edge grain can be made stronger than the wood itself. Glue does not hold well on end grain, however, for it is drawn into the wood by the open cells of end grain before it has a chance to set between the mating surfaces.

The process of gluing consists essentially of applying liquid glue to the surfaces to be fastened together and then applying pressure to hold them together until the glue has set. It normally requires several hours for glue to set and several days for some glues to become unaffected by strain. Glue does not act as a filler and cement between two surfaces; its holding power depends upon its bonding action and this works best between surfaces which are in close contact with each other.

There is much more involved in the use of glue than just spreading it on a joint and pressing the parts together. Adhesives have become an exact science and to make a strong joint in the required conditions of use requires knowledge and experience. Some of the knowledge can be obtained by study of this chapter and by consulting other sources. Experience can be acquired by practice.

Types of Adhesive

There are several kinds of glue suitable for use with wood, the most common ones being animal, casein, synthetic resin and one known generally as PVA. Each of these has special properties and no one kind meets all requirements. It is necessary to choose the glue most suited to the job to be done. Some come in ready-to-use liquid form, others require preparation and come as solids or dry powders which are mixed with water. Some are two-part liquids, ie the glue plus a chemical hardener. Most are used cold; one, once quite common, requires heating and is used hot. Glues which require preparation are, in general terms, the strongest and most enduring glues. The ready-to-use liquids have the advantage of convenience, however, and so tend to be most frequently used in the more common workshop and household situations. The white liquid glue used by many woodworkers is one such glue.

PVA (Polyvinyl Acetate)

This cold setting, ready-to-use glue is probably the most common glue for general woodworking purposes. It is in the form of a fairly thick white liquid. It has good keeping qualities if kept sealed and at room temperature. It is generally free from staining but excess glue should be wiped off as it inhibits finishing and polishing. Initially it can be wiped off work etc with a water-damp cloth but on setting becomes glass hard. Many other materials other than wood can be glued with it, including fabrics, paper, tiles etc. It gives a strong bond with wood but it is not a waterproof glue. It is sold under various trade names: Resin W, Uni-bond, Croid Fabrex, Casco PVA etc.

Synthetic Resin Glues

These completely waterproof glues are sold under various trade names of which Aerolite 300 and Cascamite are examples. Broadly speaking there are two types of glue in this group: urea-formaldehyde and phenol-formaldehyde.

Urea-formaldehyde glue is the one most suitable for small workshop use. It comes either as a two-part liquid or as a dry powder. The two-part liquid consists of the adhesive itself and a chemical hardening agent. The most common method

111

of application is to coat one mating surface with the adhesive and the other with the hardener. The adhesive will not set until it is in contact with the hardener. This is often a helpful consideration when assembling glued work. The powder form contains both adhesive and an inert hardener. The addition of water activates the hardener and a single application glue is produced. Synthetic resin glues form a strong bond and their waterproof qualities make them suitable for work exposed to dampness and even direct contact with water. They are widely employed in boat building.

Phenol-formaldehyde glues are used mainly for industrial purposes, plywood manufacture etc. Most glues of this type require hot pressing and setting temperatures which are quite critical.

Mixing a Resin Glue
Manufacturers' instructions should be followed when using glues. The dry powder form of resin glue should be mixed in a non-metal container such as plastic or glass which must be free from all traces of alkaline. Soap, soda and the residue of certain other glues such as casein glues are alkaline. Even a slight trace will retard the setting of resin glues. And use a dry spoon or scoop to take powder from the container.

Mix only as much glue as is needed for immediate use. It will not remain usable for more than a few hours. Powder and water may be measured by weight or by volume, usually in the ratio of two parts powder to one part cold water by weight or three measures of powder to one measure of water by volume. Stir until all the water is absorbed and the mixture has the consistency of smooth cream. It is then ready for use. Too much water added to the mix will result in a weaker, slower setting glue. Some add the minimum amount of water to give a thicker, creamy mix for a stronger, faster setting glue.

Utensils, fingers and work surfaces can be washed clean with warm, soapy water before the glue has set. When set it

112

becomes glass hard and can be damaging to edge cutting tools. It stains certain woods.

Casein Glues

These too are glues sold in powder form which require mixing with water before they are ready for use. Skimmed milk forms the basis of these glues. While not completely waterproof, they have some resistance to dampness. They exhibit strong bonding qualities but their disadvantage is that they are liable to stain hardwoods such as oak, mahogany etc. Non-staining glues are obtainable but even these can cause some staining and they are generally less damp resistant.

Mixing a Casein Glue

Directions for mixing a casein glue should be followed carefully. Equal measures of powder and water by volume or one part powder to two parts water by weight are the usual recommendations. Mix in a non-metallic container, and water at room temperature should be used. If the water is too cold the glue will be too thick; too warm and it will be too thin and set too quickly. Mix to a thin paste then let the mixture stand for ten to fifteen minutes. A final stir and the glue is ready for use. The glue remains usable for approximately fifteen minutes only. Utensils and work can be cleaned with water before the glue sets.

Animal Glues

These have long been the favourite type of glue of cabinet makers but modern adhesives have gradually almost replaced them. Animal glues—commonly known as Scotch glue—are strong, set quickly, flow into joints well and are stainless. Their disadvantages are that they require time and care in their preparation, must be used hot and applied very quickly. They are satisfactory only for damp-free, indoor work. Made from bones, hides and other animal waste products, they are still available and sold now in pellet form. Before use they have to be soaked in water then melted by heating. A double

113

glue pot is normally used for melting so that the glue cannot be overheated. The glue will spoil if allowed to boil. A tin can set in a pan of water may be used as a substitute glue pot.

The proper amount of water used in preparing Scotch glue varies with the glue and the kind of wood to be joined. A rough rule, by weight, is usually two parts water to one part glue for hardwoods and one and a half parts water to one part glue for softwoods. Continued or repeated heating evaporates some of the water, decreasing its strength. Thick glue prevents the parts of a joint making the close contact necessary to secure a good bond. Thin, watery glue also lacks strength. Hot Scotch glue should be of a thin syrup consistency and run freely from the brush. If it is too thick, add a little water.

General Directions for Gluing

The conditions required for using the different glues vary. But there are two basic requirements which apply to all glues:

1. The joint must fit perfectly before glue is applied.
2. The glued surfaces must be pressed together and kept under pressure, usually for several hours. This pressure time varies with room temperature, type of glue and kind of wood.

All surfaces which are to be glued must fit together tightly. When put under pressure they must touch at all points. Glue is not a space filler. It is true that if glue is thick enough, it will fill up a space in a joint, but when it hardens it will crack and the joint will not be strong. The adhesive strength which holds glue to wood is much greater than the cohesive strength which holds glue together. In other words, a thin film of glue between two well-fitting pieces of wood makes a stronger joint than a thick layer of glue. It is advisable to test the fit of all pieces by assembling them under pressure before applying any glue. This is known as a 'dry run'. If parts do not fit properly, make them do so before gluing up.

114

Applying Pressure

Pressure may be applied to glued work in a variety of ways. Cramping or clamping using 'G' cramps ('C' clamps), sash or bar cramps, vices, heavy weights, rubber bands, wedges and cords are all used to hold work together. Several holding devices may be needed to secure a job properly. It is sometimes necessary to make special fixtures to hold irregular shapes or angled joints.

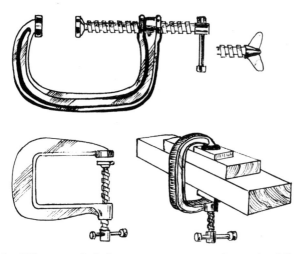

Using the 'G' cramp. It is important to protect the work whilst under pressure by means of small pieces of waste wood. A standard heavy duty cramp is shown, together with (below) a small 'long reach' cramp

Planned Gluing

To make a good, permanent glued piece of work it is necessary to plan the whole operation. If it is a large job, it should be studied and a way worked out to do the job in small units. This will make it easier to get the cramps in place properly and true up all the joints as the work progresses. For example, it would be difficult to glue together all the separate parts of a chair in one operation.

In addition to testing the fit of parts to be glued before applying glue, the dry run should also be used to plan and test the method of cramping to be used. After the glue has been

115

applied is the wrong time to discover that the cramps slip off or pull the work out of shape. In most cases it will be necessary to prepare softwood blocks or strips for use between the cramps and finished surfaces to prevent the latter from being marked by the cramps.

If a test proves that all is satisfactory, all cramps needed for the job should be adjusted so that they can be put back in place and tightened quickly and conveniently. Near at hand on the workbench should be a square, straight edge, rule, mallet, chisel, scraper and a damp cloth. The square, straight edge and rule may be needed to check the alignment and squareness of the job when cramping pressure is applied. Sometimes a tap with the mallet will help a tight joint to close up or the parts to align properly. The chisel, scraper and damp cloth are used to remove surplus glue before it hardens.

Using a PVA Glue

A PVA glue is simply used direct from its container, spread with a small brush or scraper on to one of the surfaces to be glued. It should be spread evenly using just enough glue so that a little oozes out along the joint when cramping pressure is applied. The surplus glue should be removed immediately and the surface wiped with the damp cloth. The glue is transparent on the wood but its glazed surface will not accept stain or polish. Glue which dries on the work surface will become glass hard and should be carefully removed with a chisel.

Glue exposed to the open air in a small container remains workable for up to about thirty minutes after which its adhesive qualities are impaired. Work should be kept under pressure for about one hour.

Using a Synthetic Resin Glue

When using this type of glue, the workshop and materials should be at about 21° C (70° F) or warmer. The liquid life of a normal mix is one to two hours. Less water will shorten the liquid's life, more will lengthen it.

116

The joints must fit perfectly with no rough surfaces. Use a stiff brush or spreader to apply the glue and spread a thin film on one surface only. There should be practically no oozing of glue from the joint when pressure is applied.

Cramping pressure should be applied as soon as possible and continued for five hours in the case of softwoods. Hardwoods should be kept under pressure for six hours. Five to six days are then required for the glue to develop full strength and water resistance. The job may be handled during this period but joints should not be strained or exposed to damp conditions.

Glue stains on exposed surfaces are objectionable on fine work. Unless they are carefully wiped off, synthetic resin glues may stain certain woods. One trick of the trade is to use coloured glue to match the finish of the wood. Synthetic resin glues may be coloured with a soluble acid-fast dye.

Using a Casein Glue

A job using a casein glue should be planned so that the glue can be spread, pressure applied and the alignment of the parts checked—and corrected if necessary—within about fifteen minutes. If too much time is taken, the glue may begin to set and the excess will not be squeezed from the joints, thus preventing the parts making proper contact.

Use sufficient glue for some to ooze from the joint under pressure. The surplus is wiped off with a damp cloth to prevent staining. Softwoods should be kept under cramping pressure for at least two hours, hardwoods for a minimum of four hours and preferably up to twelve. Casein glue requires nearly a week to develop full strength. Do not strain the joints until the glue is properly cured.

Some woods, eg teak, yellow pine and yew, are naturally oily. Glue does not adhere to them as well as it does to other woods. Casein is perhaps the best glue to use for joining these materials. Wiping over surfaces to be joined with a strong solution of any alkaline household cleaning substance will usually improve the glue bond.

117

Using an Animal Glue

An animal glue, such as Scotch glue, must be used hot and used quickly. When chilled or too thick, it does not penetrate into the pores of the wood and does not adhere satisfactorily. Also the glue does not squeeze out of a joint properly and prevents joint surfaces coming into close contact. The glue will later crack and the joint will come apart.

With this type of glue it is most important to have everything ready so that no time is lost when gluing up. The glue should be applied generously with a stiff brush to both surfaces to be joined. Pressure should be applied immediately, and parts checked for alignment and altered without delay if needs be. Speed is essential when using this glue. The joint must then remain undisturbed for several hours under pressure.

Surplus glue smeared on the work or squeezed out of joints is best removed with a scraper or chisel as soon as it chills and thickens. If glue is removed while it is still warm, it smears the surface; after it has thoroughly hardened it is difficult to remove without damage to the surface.

Glued Joints

All the common woodworking joints such as lap joints, mortice and tenons, dovetails etc, are secured with glue of a type suitable to the piece of work and conditions of use. In addition there are certain special joining techniques.

Gluing Boards Edge to Edge

Butt joints between the edges of two or more boards can be made stronger and more permanent by gluing than by nailing or screwing. Adjoining edges should be carefully planed along their entire length to give a true, square face. If this is well done and if the boards have been matched for figure (grain markings on the surface) the glued joints will be practically invisible. This is a most suitable method of producing wide surfaces suitable for table tops etc.

118

After applying glue, press the edges together and rub them back and forth several times. This rubs glue into the pores of the wood and improves adhesion. This type of joint is often called a rubbed joint for this reason.

There are several ways of cramping and holding boards under pressure until the glue has set. If cabinet maker's sash or bar cramps are used, a minimum of three will be required. Place two on the underside of the job towards the ends and the third on top and near the centre. The centre cramp is tightened first, then even pressure is put on the two end cramps. Avoid too much pressure or the boards may bulge. Check for flatness with a straight edge. It may be necessary, especially when gluing several boards together to obtain a wide surface, to cramp a straight-edged board across each end. Regardless of the method used, there is a tendency for long glued edges to spring apart at the ends. Greater cramping pressure should therefore be applied at the ends than at the centre.

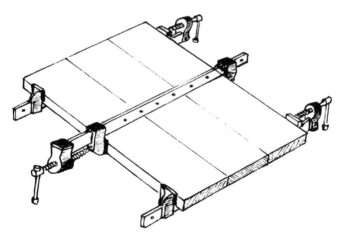

Gluing boards edge to edge using the sash cramp

If sash cramps are not available, pressure can be applied by using wooden cramps and wedge arrangements. Cramps may be made up from substantial battens a little over the width of the boards to be joined. Blocks with an inside sloping face are screwed to each end of the batten to leave a small gap between the block and the edge of the glued boards. Wedges which match the slope of the end blocks are then tapped in to place to secure the work. Another method makes use of a pivoted frame. When the ends of this are tapped with a hammer, the frame slants, pivoting as shown in the illustration, and making the frame fit tightly.

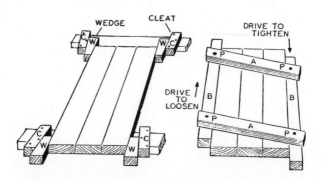

Cramping with cleats and wedges and with a pivoted frame

Gluing a Panel

If a panel is formed of more than one piece, the pieces should be glued together using the rubbed joint just described. However, no glue should be used to fasten the panel into the frame in which it fits. The panel itself should be free to expand and contract in accordance with changes in moisture in the atmosphere.

Gluing an Irregular Shape

Cramps cannot be applied directly to some irregular shapes and curved surfaces. It is necessary to make special blocks when this occurs. The blocks are made to fit the shaped surface and at the same time provide parallel surfaces for the jaws of the cramp so that the jaws may be drawn up tightly. Cramping blocks should always be of softwood.

When cramping up especially awkward shapes, blocks may

be temporarily glued to the work. Glue the blocks to the work with paper between. When dry the blocks are easily knocked off and the paper scraped off the surface.

Gluing a Mitre
Picture frames, mirrors and small panelled cabinet doors mitred at the corners cannot be drawn together with ordinary cramps. Special mitre cramps must be used or a fixture

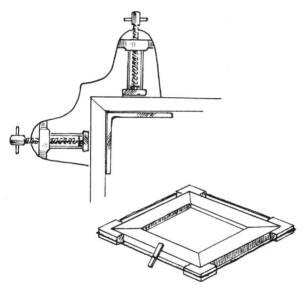

Gluing mitres. Above are mitre cramps, four of which are needed to glue up a frame. The simple device below is relatively cheap and quite effective

consisting of a board to which four battens are fixed at right angles to each other may be used. Double wedges are driven between the battens and the glued frame. Alternatively a simple cramping device consisting of four right-angled blocks and a length of cord works quite well. A block is placed over each corner and the cord tied round, resting in grooves on the outside of the blocks. A short piece of stick is used to twist the cord and thus apply pressure to the corner blocks.

121

Gluing a Dowel Joint

In order to make a strong joint all dowels must fit snugly into their corresponding holes. The holes should be slightly deeper than half the length of the dowel so that the adjoining surfaces come together. Cut a small groove the full length of the dowel (use a tenon saw or a 'V'-shaped gouge) so that air and excess glue may escape when the dowel is forced into its hole. Point or round the end of the dowel slightly so that it will enter the hole more easily.

8
Drills and Drilling

When a hole is to be drilled or bored in wood, the size, location and purpose of the hole determine what kind of drilling tool will be needed and whether an auger bit, centre bit, expansive bit, Forstner bit, flat bit or twist drill should be used.

For drilling holes by hand the carpenter's brace, hand drill or wheel brace may be used. In addition, of course, the power drill can be used. This is discussed at length in the next chapter.

Braces

A brace is a crank used to hold and turn bits and drills when boring holes in wood. There are two basic types: the rachet brace and the plain brace. Both have a metal frame and the best types have a ball-bearing head and handle usually of wood, and a chuck. This is designed to hold square shanked bits in 'V'-shaped grooves in its twin jaws. Some braces are obtainable which have a four-jaw chuck. This will accept both square and round shanked bits. It is in the drive to the chuck where the two types differ. The rachet, which may be locked out of use or made to operate in either direction, makes it possible to use the brace in confined spaces where there is not enough room to turn the brace through its full sweep of 360°. With the rachet 'on', the handle of the brace can be turned backwards without moving the bit. Braces are obtainable in several sizes, each 'size' being the diameter in inches of the arc made by the handle as it is revolved. This is known as the *sweep* of the brace.

123

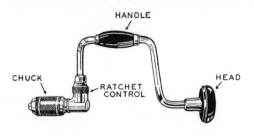

A bit brace

Hand Drills

Also known as the wheel brace, the hand drill has a cranked handle attached to a toothed drive wheel. One or two smaller bevelled gears engage with the drive wheel to rotate the chuck at right angles to the plane in which the cranked handle is turned. The tool is held by a fixed handle gripped in one hand whilst the other hand turns the crank. The chuck, which is three jawed and self centring, is tightened by hand. Standard models take straight shanked drills up to $\frac{1}{4}$in (6mm) in diameter.

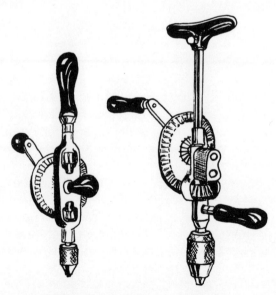

A hand drill and the larger breast drill

124

A larger version, known as the breast drill, will take drills up to $\frac{1}{2}$in (12mm) in diameter. This drill is intended for much heavier work and a curved plate replaces the fixed handle so that the user may lean against it to increase pressure.

In general use the brace is best for boring large diameter or deep holes in wood while the hand drill is more suited for making smaller holes such as those needed for wood screws etc. The hand drill can also be used, with suitable drill, for drilling light metals etc.

Bits and Drills

The choice of bits and drills for use with both tools is a wide one. Bits intended only for use in braces fitted with the standard two-jaw chuck have a square tang at the end of the shank which is efficiently held in the chuck jaws. Bits and drills with round, parallel shanks right to the end are for use in hand drills and power operated tools whose chucks are suited to this shape of shank.

Auger Bits

The common auger bits are square tanged and sized by $\frac{1}{16}$in (1·5mm) and are made to bore holes from $\frac{1}{4}$in (6mm) up to $1\frac{1}{2}$in (38mm) in diameter. Alternatively they may be in metric sizes. Special purpose bits to bore holes up to 2in (50mm) in diameter are obtainable but are not readily available.

The size of an auger in fractions of an inch or in millimetres is usually stamped on its shank. Sometimes a number is used to indicate the diameter of the hole that the auger will bore in 16ths of an inch. For example, a no 4 auger will bore a hole $\frac{4}{16}$ths of an inch in diameter, or, in other words, $\frac{1}{4}$in (6mm). A $\frac{1}{2}$in (12mm) bit is marked with an 8 and so on.

The cutting parts of an auger bit are the screw or lead screw, the spurs or nibs and the lips, cutters or routers.

The screw centres the bit and draws it into the wood. Screws may be made fast, medium or slow. The fast pitch has a coarse thread and cuts fast, the slow pitch a fine thread

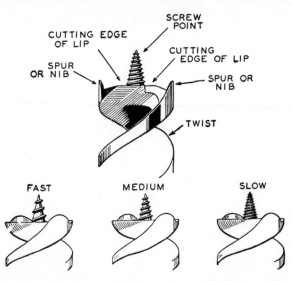

The cutting end of an auger bit. The screw centres the bit and draws it into the wood. The spurs or nibs score the circle and the lips cut out the wood. The pitch of the screw determines the cutting speed of the bit

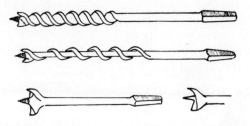

Types of bit. Top, the double twist or Jennings pattern auger bit. Middle, the solid centre auger bit. Below, the centre bit and (right) the old-type centre bit

which cuts more slowly. A medium pitch screw is the most serviceable for all-round work.

The spurs or nibs score the circumference of the hole and sever the fibres of the wood to prevent splintering. The lips or routers cut out the waste from the hole while the twist or thread of the bit lifts the shavings clear of the hole.

Two types of auger bit are in general use by woodworkers: the double twist or Jennings pattern and the solid centre. The double twist cuts more smoothly and accurately, but the solid

126

centre is much stronger. Extra long bits are usually of the solid centre type.

Dowel Bits

These are short, double twist, Jennings-pattern auger bits. About half the length of ordinary augers, they are, as their name implies, used for boring the holes for dowel pins used in jointing. They are also available with straight shanks.

Centre Bits

Two types are available, one with a triangular centre point, one cutting edge or lip and a simple, pointed spur. This type of bit does not pull itself into the wood and as a consequence much pressure is required when using it. The second type, the improved centre bit, has a lead screw centre, a single helical twist giving two cutting edges and a single spur. Its cutting action is similar to the auger bit but, without the supportive thread behind the cutting edges, it tends to wander off centre in use. It is not suitable for boring deep holes. It is used principally to bore shallow holes or through thin sections of wood. In the latter case bore from both sides as described later. They are normally supplied with square tanged shanks.

Forstner Bits

These have no lead screw, spurs or twist. The cutting is done by two lips or nibs and a circular steel rim. Forstner bits, which are available with square tang or straight shanks, cut very accurately and leave flat-bottomed holes. They are made in sizes up to 2in (50mm) in diameter.

Forstner bits have special uses and advantages over other types of bit. These are:

1. They will bore equally well in end grain and across the grain.
2. They will bore holes which overlap. This makes them particularly useful for removing waste wood from recesses, mortices etc.

3. They will bore holes in thin wood near an end which the screw of an auger bit would split.
4. They will not wander off centre by following the grain.
5. They can be used to bore holes at an angle regardless of the direction of the grain.

They are not recommended for boring deep holes, but if the bit is removed at intervals to clear the waste, holes twice the depth of the diameter of the bit is possible. When boring right through a piece of wood, a block of waste wood should be clamped to the back to prevent splitting as the bit cuts through. Because it has no lead screw, the Forstner bit must be used under pressure in order to cut into the work.

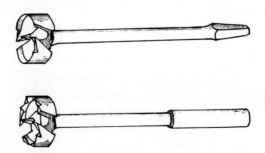

The Forstner bit and the saw toothed Forstner type

Saw Tooth Bits
Similar in construction to the Forstner bit, this has a series of saw-like teeth instead of the plain rim. These cut before the cutting lips come into contact with the wood. They will bore accurate, deep holes even in end grain.

Expansive Bits
When large holes are to be bored, a cabinet-maker or carpenter may use an expansive or extension bit. This fits into the brace, having, usually a square tang. Its cutting action is similar to an improved centre bit but it has an adjustable cutting blade which can be set to bore holes of any size within its range. Two sizes are available: one which will bore holes

128

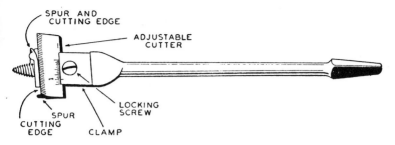

SPUR AND
CUTTING EDGE

ADJUSTABLE
CUTTER

SPUR

CUTTING
EDGE

LOCKING
SCREW

CLAMP

The extension or expansive bit can be adjusted to bore holes of any diameter within its range

from ½in (12mm) to 1½in (38mm) and a larger size to bore holes ⅞in (22mm) up to 3in (76mm) in diameter.

The adjustable spur and cutting edge is fastened to the shank by a screw passing through a small steel clamp. Loosening this screw makes it possible to move the spur and alter the size of the bit. The screw must be firmly tightened again so that the spur cannot slip in use. The accuracy of the adjustment should always be tested on a piece of waste wood.

As with other bits, boring right through a piece of wood may cause splintering and the procedure outlined for boring through with auger bits should be followed when using the expansive bit.

Flat Bits
Otherwise known as the spade bit, the flat bit is an inexpensive bit useful for boring holes in wood and in man-made composite boards. It was developed for use in the power drill and is only efficient when used at the high speeds produced by such tools.

Countersink Bits
These bits are used to shape the top of a screw hole so that the head of a countersunk screw may be driven flush with, or slightly below, the surface of the work. There are two types. One is known as the rose head; the other is the snail-horn pattern. Both function in the same way but the snail horn is somewhat better for hardwood. Both are available with square or round shanks.

129

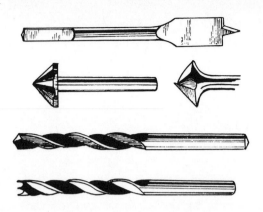

Bits and drills. From top to bottom: the flat bit, for use in electric power drills; two types of countersink bit; a common type of twist drill; the lip and spur twist drill

Twist Drills

Sometimes called Morse drills after their inventor, twist drills have double helical flutes running into a straight or parallel shank. For boring wood the two cutting edges or lips are usually ground to an angle of about 45°. Twist drills for wood are of carbon steel and are not tempered hard enough to make holes in metal. Drills of high speed steel can be used to make holes in both wood and metal, although for drilling metal the cutting edges should be ground to an angle greater than 45°.

Used mainly to make holes for screws when fitting hinges etc, twist bits are available singly or in sets sized in $\frac{1}{32}$in from $\frac{1}{16}$in (1·5mm) to $\frac{1}{2}$in (12mm). Metric sizes run from 1mm to 13mm, and numbered drills are obtainable also.

Correctly used in either hand or power operated drills, the smaller sizes produce neat, accurate holes in both softwood and hardwood. Small holes in softwood may also be made with a bradawl (see p 99).

A special type of twist drill specifically designed for use in wood is the lip and spur twist drill. This has a triangular centre point and short spurs for accurate centring and cutting.

130

Using a Brace

Many a man who considers himself handy with tools bores crooked holes. Boring a hole which both starts and ends where it should is easy if the bit or drill is 'sighted' from two points 90° apart. Sight when beginning the hole and again at intervals during the work; it takes only a few seconds.

First make certain that the bit is held securely in the chuck. Then go to work. Hold the head of the brace with the palm and fingers of the left hand and turn the handle with the right. Of course, if you are left handed this position will be reversed. At a bench it is usual to hold the brace and bit horizontally if possible (unless boring at an angle). A horizontal position

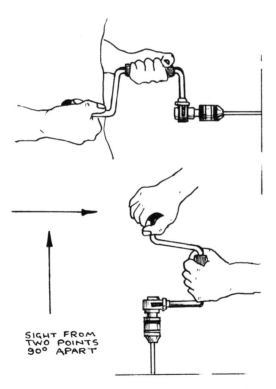

SIGHT FROM
TWO POINTS
90° APART

Using a brace. Keep the tool in the correct position by 'sighting' during both horizontal and vertical boring

131

helps the eye to sight the tool more accurately at right angles to the surface of the wood to be bored.

The centre of the hole to be bored should be located and marked with a bradawl. The point of the drill or bit is then placed in this mark. Then, the handle of the brace is turned slowly in a clockwise direction, and at the same time pressure is exerted on the head of the brace. When boring softwoods the drill or bit will enter quite easily; for hardwoods more pressure is needed. When using auger bits the pressure of the hand and the pull of the lead screw on the bit both combine to force the bit into the wood. As soon as the spurs of the bit touch the work, the eyes are brought down to that level where the auger can be sighted from two positions. Sight from one position to check that the brace and bit are perpendicular to the work in one plane and the same with respect to another plane at right angles to the first—in other words, from above and from one side. Correct any error and, with the brace held steady, continue boring.

If you are not sure of your eye judgement, test for accuracy with a small try square.

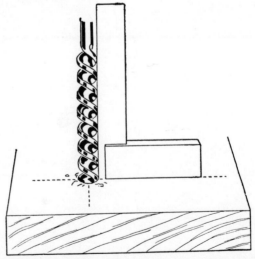

Boring perpendicular to a surface. Check the position of the auger with a try square until your eye is trained

When the spurs and cutting edge have entered the wood, sight the work once more and again correct any error. Continue boring until the auger reaches the desired depth. If boring right through, stop boring when the auger is almost through. At this point turn the brace slowly and with less pressure. Watch for the point of the lead screw to come through on the underside of the work. As soon as it does, stop turning the brace. Remove all pressure from the brace and turn the handle slowly in the opposite direction (anti-clockwise) so as to back out the lead screw and withdraw the bit as soon as it is free. Now turn the work over, place the point of the bit in the visible hole and bore through from the opposite side.

Boring from one side only splits the wood as the bit breaks through. Boring from two sides results in a smooth, clean-edged hole. If you have sighted the auger accurately, the hole will have come through where you wanted it to.

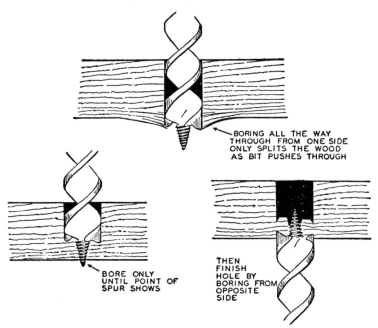

BORING ALL THE WAY THROUGH FROM ONE SIDE ONLY SPLITS THE WOOD AS BIT PUSHES THROUGH

BORE ONLY UNTIL POINT OF SPUR SHOWS

THEN FINISH HOLE BY BORING FROM OPPOSITE SIDE

Bore from both sides to prevent the bit from breaking through

Boring from one side only can be done without danger of splintering when the bit comes through by clamping a piece of waste wood tightly on the back of the work in such a position that the bit will cut into it as it completes the hole in the work.

Boring at an Angle

Boring holes at an angle is no more difficult than boring them at right angles to a surface.

If the angle is only a slight one, there will be no difficulty in starting the bit and getting it to bite into the wood. It is a good plan to lay the angle out on a piece of thin wood and use this as a sighting guide.

When a hole is to be drilled at a considerable angle, it is sometimes difficult to start the bit without some additional help. A simple guide can be made by boring a vertical hole through a block of wood using the same size bit that is to be used to bore the angled hole. The bottom of the block is then sawn off to suit the required angle and clamped to the work piece. The centre of the hole in the bottom of the block must be directly over the centre of the hole to be bored. If the bit is then inserted in the hole in the block, you can bore the hole while the block holds the bit at the proper angle and prevents it from slipping.

It is easy to calculate the required angle of the bottom of the block. Deduct from 90° the angle of the hole to be bored. What remains is the angle the bottom of the block should have. For example, if a hole is to be bored at an angle of 60°, deduct 60 from 90 and the answer is 30. The angle of the bottom of the block is cut at 30°.

Using a Hand Drill

To fit a drill into the chuck, take hold of the drive handle and, while holding it still, turn the chuck anticlockwise to open the jaws. Insert a drill and tighten it by turning clockwise. Check that the drill is central in the chuck.

When drilling with a twist drill it is necessary to hold the driving mechanism firmly and drive the drill perfectly straight with steady but light pressure. Otherwise the drill may be bent or broken. The shank of a drill is soft and is able to bend but the body of the drill is tempered and will snap off if sufficiently strained. This is especially true of drills of small diameter.

Inserting a drill into the chuck

When driven steadily, a twist drill will bite into wood quite quickly but, if it is pushed ahead too fast, the chips will not clear properly. When this occurs the chips clog in the drill flutes and the drill may stick and break or become hot. It may become hot enough to spoil its own temper. Such a drill will no longer hold a keen cutting edge.

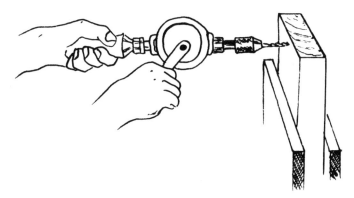

Boring a hole with the hand drill

Withdraw the drill several times to clear the chips from its flutes, especially when drilling hardwoods or resinous softwoods. If the flutes are jammed with chips, the drill squeals as it revolves. The drill should be withdrawn and cleared immediately. Continue to rotate the drill in a clockwise direction as it is withdrawn—*do not* attempt to just pull it out.

The hand drill and suitable twist drills are especially useful whenever a good job of setting a screw is to be done. Two sizes of drill are usually necessary for this job to bore pilot and clearance holes (see p 104 for full details). Special combination drills matched to the different screw sizes are available. These bore pilot and clearance holes, and countersink in one operation.

To bore accurately to a predetermined depth a special depth gauge can be fitted to the drill. A simple, temporary method is to mark the drill with a piece of adhesive tape or something similar.

9

Power Tools and Attachments

The introduction of hand-held power tools has been the cause of a minor revolution in woodworking over the past few years. The portable electric drill, with its multitude of attachments and accessories, together with the many special single-function power tools available, are now widely used and accepted by many. Their value in terms of getting things done more quickly, sometimes more accurately and certainly with greater ease cannot be denied.

The earliest portable power tool was the single-speed electric drill intended solely for drilling holes in wood and light metals. Gradual development led to the use of more powerful motors and variable speed gearboxes until now the once simple electric drill has become the power unit of a veritable multi-purpose tool. With the addition of various attachments the worker may not only drill holes but also sand, shape, saw and joint his work with the minimum of effort.

Although most electric drills are similar in appearance there are important differences between many of them. Choosing the right one depends on how you intend to use it. Three main points must be considered: how powerful it should be, what size chuck is needed and what speed, or speeds, is required.

A drill's power is generally given in watts—the higher the stated wattage the more powerful the motor. For general purpose woodworking a 300 to 400 watt motor is adequate. This is suitable for all drilling jobs and occasional use with a variety of attachments. Drills designated 'heavy-duty' have more powerful motors and are more suitable for prolonged and heavy work.

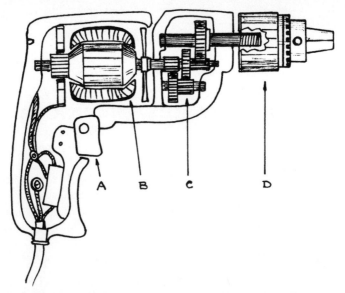

Section through a typical electric drill. A trigger switch; B motor; C Reduction gears; D chuck

Chuck capacity refers to the maximum size of drill shank that can be accepted. Common sizes are $\frac{1}{4}$in (6mm), $\frac{5}{16}$in (8mm) and $\frac{1}{2}$in (12mm). Heavy-duty drills have chucks of larger capacity. Normally, the larger the chuck the more powerful the drill but this may not always be the case so check it. Small-capacity chucks can be used to bore larger holes by the use of drills with reduced shanks but care should be taken not to overload the motor.

The speed of a drill should be matched to the work it is doing. For drilling up to about $\frac{3}{8}$in (9mm) diameter in most woods, a speed of between 2,500 and 3,000 revolutions per minute (rpm) is required. This speed range is also adequate for most sawing and sanding attachments. For drilling larger holes, especially in hardwood, a slower speed is both desirable and safer. Somewhere around 1,000 rpm is recommended. This speed is also about right for drilling holes into masonry or brickwork and is therefore useful for those fixing jobs which always seem to turn up. A tungsten-tipped masonry drill should be used for this work.

Two-speed and four-speed drills are available which cover this range of speeds, the correct speed being selected before use by means of a knob or key button. Variable speed drills are also available. These have an electronic switch trigger which allows the motor to rotate faster as more pressure is applied by the operator.

Using an Electric Drill
The standard chuck takes all drills and bits with straight or parallel shanks. To fit a drill into the chuck open the chuck jaws by turning, by hand, anticlockwise. Insert the drill shank and close the chuck by turning it clockwise, checking that the drill is central. The chuck is tightened and opened by means of a chuck key.

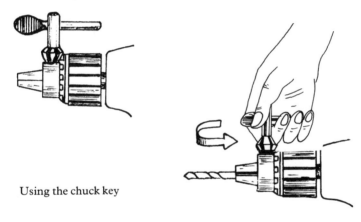

Using the chuck key

Most drills are of the pistol grip type with the on/off trigger incorporated in the grip. This allows the drill to be used with one hand. A detachable side handle may be fitted to help steady the drill; otherwise the body of the tool is grasped for extra support. With the trigger pressed, a lock button can be used to give continuous running—an essential feature when using the drill to power certain bench attachments.

When drilling holes make sure the workpiece is firmly held. Do not hold small items in the hand but secure them in a vice or with a clamp. The drill will often 'bite' better when

139

starting to make a hole if its centre is first marked with a punch or a bradawl. Place the tip of the drill on the mark, squeeze the trigger and apply gentle pressure. Do not force the drill to cut too quickly but keep up a steady pressure.

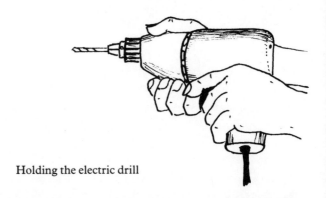

Holding the electric drill

Large holes should be started by making a small pilot hole first and enlarging this to the required size. When drilling deep holes the drill should be withdrawn periodically to clear the waste wood and prevent clogging. When drilling right through a piece of wood, a controlled finish, using less pressure, will avoid splintering the wood around the exit hole. When withdrawing a drill, keep the power on and the drill turning until it is clear of the hole. This clears the waste and prevents the drill sticking in the hole. Small drills especially are easily broken if this is not done.

Drill Attachments

By means of various attachments the electric drill's use is considerably extended. A number of manufacturers make attachments, some for specific models, others with more universal application. Check before buying that an attachment will fit your particular drill.

Drill Stands
There are two types of stand: one which holds the drill in a

140

vertical position and one which holds it horizontally. The vertical stand enables the drill to be used as a drill press or pillar drill. Its base can be fixed to a bench and the drill, held in a secure cradle, is lowered and raised by means of a simple sprung lever. The horizontal stand holds the drill when using attachments such as grinding wheels, sanding discs etc.

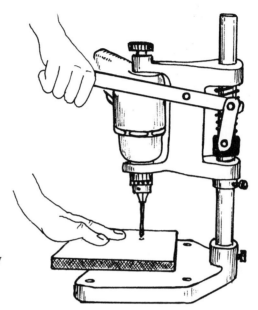

Using the electric drill. Here the drill is securely held in a vertical stand which converts the tool into a small pillar drill

Grinding Wheels
Small abrasive wheels of various grades or grits can be used in the electric drill. Quite useful for regrinding edge tools and screwdriver blades, a short spindle which attaches to the grinding wheel is gripped in the chuck of the drill. The direction of rotation should be down towards the user and the items for grinding held to the bottom of the rotating wheel.

Sanding

Smoothing wood by hand is a time-consuming job and the electric drill has been readily adapted to this work with

141

varying degrees of success. Several types of drill-driven sanders are available.

Disc Sanders

The most simple is the disc sander, a flexible rubber pad, 4in (102mm) to 6in (152mm) in diameter. This has either a plain or a threaded shank projecting from its centre, the first fitting directly into the drill chuck. The other screws into the drill spindle after removal of the chuck. Paper- or cloth-backed abrasive discs are fixed to the rubber pad by means of a flat-headed screw and shaped washer. A recess in the pad keeps these below the working surface. Pressed metal discs with grains of tungsten carbide bonded to the surface are also available.

In use the abrasive disc should be held lightly against the surface to be sanded and at a shallow angle (about 12°) so that only one side of the disc is in contact. Hold the tool in both hands and work across the surface with the tilt in the direction of movement. Disc sanders can be quite fierce in use and can easily leave nasty score marks on a workpiece. They are perhaps best used only for rough work.

Bench Sanders

Very useful for shaping work, the drill must be held in a horizontal stand secured to the bench when using this

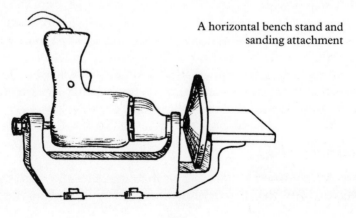

A horizontal bench stand and sanding attachment

attachment. It consists of a metal table—usually arranged so that it can be tilted at an angle if required—which fits to the drill stand, and a flat metal disc which is gripped in the drill chuck. A paper-backed abrasive disc is stuck to the face of the metal disc with a suitable adhesive.

The workpiece should be held against the down side of the disc to keep it firm against the table and kept moving. This evens out wear on the disc. Too much pressure will leave burn marks on the work. The table is checked for being square with the face of the disc by using a try square before switching on. It can then be used to square off ends or make mitres of any angle by means of a mitre gauge which fits into a groove across the table.

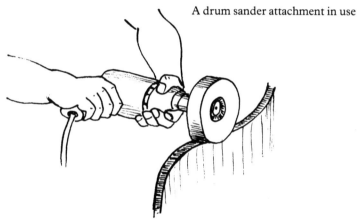

A drum sander attachment in use

Drum Sanders

This type of sander can be used with the drill secured in the horizontal stand or held freehand. This useful attachment consists of a thick plastic foam drum around a metal centre and shank which fits into the drill chuck. A continuous band of abrasive paper fits closely over the foam drum. The resilience of the foam allows the drum to shape itself to the contours of a piece of work. Hold the drill, or the workpiece, firmly to avoid any tendency to bounce. This can score the work and tear the abrasive band. Damaged or worn bands are easily replaceable.

Orbital Sanders

These attachments have a flat, rectangular base pad across which is stretched a piece of abrasive paper held by spring clips or a toothed clamp at each end. The mechanism causes the pad to oscillate with tiny, rapid, circular movements and the tool is moved over the surface of the work by the operator. Sanding is best done in a series of overlapping parallel lines, rather like ironing a shirt. Work with the grain, holding the tool at a slight angle to its direction of travel. Do not press down too hard, let the weight of the sander do most of the work but keep it moving all the time. A final light sanding by hand will produce a good finish.

Sawing

Two types of saw attachment can be powered by the electric drill: circular saws and sabre saws.

Circular Saws

These consist of a metal housing which incorporates a guide handle and a fixed upper blade guard. An adjustable sole plate provides depth of cut and angled-cut facilities. A spring-loaded lower blade guard gives the user some protection from

The circular saw attachment. The saw blade is bolted into place and tightened with a spanner

the blade before starting and after completing a cut. The drill, with its chuck removed, is fixed into this housing, a suitable saw blade being secured to the threaded drill spindle by means of a special hexagonal bolt.

Using a Circular Saw
Material to be cut should be held securely, with sufficient clearance below for the protruding saw blade. With the power on, the saw is held firmly in both hands and fed into the wood with a steady pressure. If this is done too slowly, the blade will overheat; if it is done too quickly, the motor will overload. Do not force the saw or twist the blade. The noise of the motor will tell you if you are doing it right or wrong.

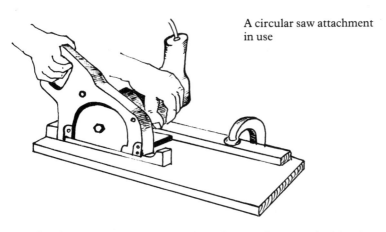

A circular saw attachment in use

A further accessory, a saw-bench attachment, holds the drill-powered saw in an upside down position with its blade protruding through a slot. This enables the portable tool to be used as a fixed table saw. Rebates and housing grooves may be cut with the saw by setting the blade to the required depth and using an adjustable fence.

Sabre Saws
The second type of saw is known as the sabre saw or sometimes the jig saw. This attachment converts the rotary

motion of the drill into a reciprocal movement to give a short but rapid up-and-down cutting stroke. A wide range of blades enables the saw to be used to cut a variety of materials. The main virtue of this tool is that its narrow blades allow it to be used to cut curved as well as straight lines, both internally and externally.

Using the sabre saw attachment to cut a curved opening in a board

Using a Sabre Saw

First secure the material to be cut to give clearance for the protruding blade. To start an external cut, ie one from an edge, first rest the tip of the sole plate or shoe on the material opposite the cutting line. Switch on and with a steady downward and forward pressure push the blade into the work. Do not force the cut; listen to the noise of the motor. Straight cuts can be made alongside a guide batten; curved cuts are done freehand on the waste side of the guide line. Do not attempt to cut too tight a curve as this will strain the blade.

Internal cuts, ie those in the centre of a workpiece, are easiest started through a hole drilled into the waste side of the cutting line. With practice a technique known as plunge cutting can be used. For this the tool is tilted forward and then brought back so that the moving blade is slowly lowered

into the wood until vertical. The saw is then moved forward
to make the cut.

Jointing

Attachments which enable the electric drill to make joints
include a comb-jointing attachment and a dovetailer. In
addition the circular saw can be used to cut the tenons of
mortice and tenon joints while the drill is helpful in removing
waste wood from the mortice slot. The drill, used with a
standard dowelling jig, enables this joint to be made also.

Comb Joints

The attachment for making these handy but time-consuming
joints consists of a horizontal bench stand with a table
assembly and blade guard. A circular saw blade is fitted to the
drill, held on a short shaft or arbor between two bevelled
washers known as 'wobble washers'. In use the blade wobbles
slightly from side to side to give the required width of cut.
Adjustable slides on the table assembly control the depth of
cut and give accurate spacing of the individual joint tongues.
Considerable care is needed to set these but once that is done
they are held securely with clamping screws and no further
adjustment should be necessary.

Mortice and Tenon Joints

To cut a tenon with the saw attachment the workpiece is first
cut to length and squared off. After marking out the tenon one
of two methods may be used to cut it. In the first the saw blade
is adjusted to the depth of the tenon and, using the guide
fence, the shoulders of the tenon are cut accurately to the
marked line. Blade and fence are then reset to the length of the
tenon and the workpiece held on end whilst the vertical cuts
are made. A simple jig can be made for holding purposes.

In the second method no vertical cuts are made. The
shoulders are first cut as before, then further cross cuts are
made parallel to these and overlapping to remove the

147

remaining waste wood. Lap joints can be cut in the same way.

To make a mortice, drill out the waste wood from the marked mortice slot using a drill slightly smaller than the slot width. Complete the work by chiselling. With the drill held in a vertical stand, very accurate mortices can be cut by this method.

Dowel Joints

The electric drill, used in conjunction with a dowelling jig, enables this type of joint to be made accurately and easily. Dowelling jigs, which are not specifically a power-drill attachment and can be used with a hand drill, consist usually of hardened steel bushes held in an adjustable carrier. This can be clamped in position onto each piece to be joined, enabling matching holes to be drilled with accuracy.

Wood Turning

A small lathe driven by an electric drill extends the use of this versatile tool even further. The bed of the lathe consists of a pressed steel channel which carries the adjustable tail stock and tool rest, and a standard horizontal stand which holds the drill and forms a fixed head stock. In place of the drill chuck may be fixed either a pronged driving dog for turning between centres or a small face plate.

A multi-speed or a variable speed drill is required for wood turning. As in normal lathe work turning speeds must be varied to match the work being done. Bearing in mind the limitations which such a lathe must have in comparison with a

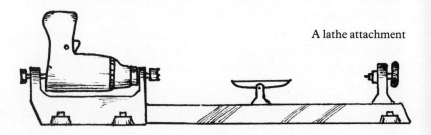

A lathe attachment

148

larger, purpose-made machine, quite good results are possible with this attachment. Normal lathe techniques and tools are used.

Single Function Power Tools

Two major criticisms of the electric drill and its various attachments are that changing from one function to another is time-consuming and that for some jobs the power and speed of the drill are unsuitable. It is true that the attachment fitted never seems to be the one needed next and that some attachments prove to be a disappointment in use. Single function or integral power tools solve both these problems. Their advantages lie in the fact that they are always ready for immediate use and, being purpose-made, are capable of doing a better job than many drill attachments.

Single function tools are powered by a motor housed in a moulded casing integral with the tool itself. An on/off switch may be incorporated into the handle or located on the motor housing. Some integral tools have motors similar in power and performance to those fitted into electric drills and these are generally only capable of similar work. Others, however, are of much more robust construction and are driven by more powerful motors. These tools are designated 'heavy-duty' or 'industrial' pattern and are more expensive but give more scope and greater staying power.

Instructions for the use of single function tools are generally the same as those given for corresponding drill attachments. See individual manufacturers' directions for details.

Safety

Power tools use electricity which is itself potentially dangerous and in use revolve at high speed. Care should be taken when operating them. Keep loose clothing etc away from moving parts. Eyes should be protected by wearing goggles. Where guards are provided on a machine always make sure they are in place and functioning properly. Always follow the safety advice given by the manufacturer when using specific attachments. And most important, before making any adjustment, removing chucks, changing attachments, fitting saw blades etc, always remove the plug from the power point to avoid accidental starting.

Make sure the electrical circuit in use is adequately fused and that where necessary the tool is properly earthed. Many electrical tools are double insulated and do not require an earth wire but check this. Check the cable and any extension lead which connects the tool to the power supply at regular intervals and keep them in good condition. Do not carry the tool by the cable and keep it away from moving parts and sharp tools.

Power tool motors are fan cooled and slots in the motor housing allow air to enter. These should be kept free from dust and not covered during use.

10
Smoothing and Finishing

When a job of woodworking has been completed, it is usually given a finish, meaning a protective and often decorative coating of varnish, wax, stain, lacquer or paint. Before any finishing coat can be successfully applied, however, all tool marks, scratches etc must normally be removed and the surface of the work made smooth. On fine woodwork final smoothing operations are done by hand with scrapers and abrasive papers.

Scrapers and Scraping

Two types of scraper for smoothing work are both known as the cabinet scraper. One is an iron-bodied tool with a scraper blade; the other a simple but effective flexible piece of tool steel held in the hand. Both do their work because their cutting edges are turned to form what is known as a hook or hooked edge.

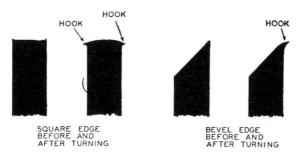

HOOK

HOOK

HOOK

SQUARE EDGE
BEFORE AND
AFTER TURNING

BEVEL EDGE
BEFORE AND
AFTER TURNING

The hooked edges of scraper blades

151

Double-handed Cabinet Scrapers

Also known as the scraper plane, the double-handed cabinet scraper has a double-sided, bevelled blade set in an iron frame with two 'wing' handles. In appearance it resembles a large spokeshave with a wide, flat sole through which the steeply angled blade protrudes. This type of scraper takes a much thinner shaving than a plane and is used only on flat surfaces after they have been planed or on surfaces that are difficult to plane properly because of irregular grain. The tool is used in both hands, the sole of the scraper lying squarely on the work surface. It may be either pulled or pushed but is probably most often pushed.

The cabinet scraper. This tool takes a finer cut than a plane and is used for fine finishing and to remove marks left by a plane

The blade is held in place by a clamp plate and two clamp screws. A central adjustable thumbscrew gives to the blade a slight curvature and alters the cut of the scraper. The blade can be removed from the body by loosening the clamp and adjusting screws. A new blade is inserted from the bottom, between the body and the clamp plate with the bevel side towards the adjusting thumbscrew.

The blade is adjusted so that it is parallel to the bottom of the scraper body by placing the latter on a flat wood surface and pressing the blade down lightly against the wood. The clamp screws are then tightened to hold it in place and the adjusting screw is tightened until it is just touching the blade. At this stage a trial cut should be made. If the scraper does not cut a nice thin shaving, tighten the adjusting screw a little. If one corner of the blade projects further than the other, slack off (a little) the clamp screws and draw it back by tapping the side of the blade near the top.

Hand Cabinet Scrapers

The hand scraper, also known as the bench scraper, produces finer shavings than the two-handed version. It can also be used on both flat and curved surfaces. The common form of hand scraper is a rectangle of high-tempered steel varying in width from 2in (50mm) to 3in (76mm) and in length from 4in (102mm) to 6in (152mm). Curved forms, called moulding scrapers, are also made for scraping shaped surfaces.

Most hand scrapers have square edges but some have bevelled edges. A square edge makes a flatter and smoother

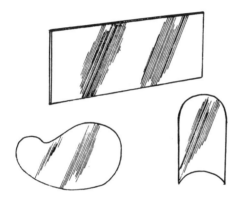

Hand scrapers. These steel blades remove finer shavings than the cabinet scraper and may be used for both flat and curved surfaces. Moulding scrapers are made especially for curves of a small radius

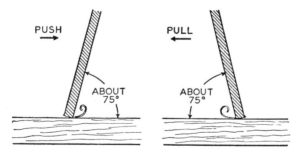

The cutting angle of a hand scraper. The blade of a hand scraper must be held to the work at an angle of approximately 75°. The correct angle will depend upon how much turn is given to the edge when it is sharpened, and can be determined by feel. Use the angle at which the scraper cuts best

surface but does not cut as fast as a scraper with a bevelled edge. A square edge also tends to get dull quicker.

A hand scraper is grasped by the fingers of both hands, the thumbs pressed low down and at the centre of the blade to produce a slight curve to the blade. Varying this pressure and so altering the amount of curve serves to localise the cut. The control comes entirely from the fingers and thumbs. The angle between the blade and the work should be about 75°. A chattering blade means it is being held too straight. It may be either pulled or pushed as the grain of the wood requires. Pushed away from the worker is probably the better of the two ways.

Cabinet scrapers of both types, in spite of their name, should cut and not merely scrape. They should take off a thin, even shaving, removing the slight ridges which may be left by a plane. Dust instead of shavings indicates a dull blade.

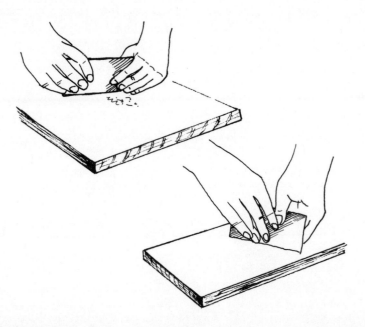

Pushing is the usual way to use the hand scraper (above) but it may also be pulled to good effect (below)

Sharpening a Scraper Blade

If you watch an experienced craftsman using a scraper, you will see him occasionally renew the edge of his blade with a burnishing tool. A burnisher, or ticketer as it is sometimes called, is a round or oval rod of tool steel, hardened and polished to a smooth surface. It is about 5in (127mm) long and fitted into a hardwood handle. It is this tool which, when rubbed hard against the edge of a scraper blade, produces the characteristic hooked edge which does the cutting. If a burnisher is not available the back of a gouge makes a good substitute.

A burnisher—used to produce the hooked edge on scraper blades

Burnishing a Scraper Blade

The cutting edge of a scraper blade can be renewed several times by a few strokes of the burnisher. The blade is first laid flat on the end of the bench and the burnisher rubbed firmly four or five times along the edge to be sharpened. Then the blade is clamped low down in the vice. Holding the burnisher handle in one hand and its tip in the other, draw the burnisher firmly towards yourself along the scraper's edge using a sliding stroke. Draw the burnisher the full length of the blade; a drop of oil helps reduce friction. For a square edge, for the first stroke the burnisher should be held at 90° to the face of the upright blade. Thereafter, tilt the burnisher slightly and gradually until after several more strokes it is at an angle of about 85°. In this manner the edge is pressed out and turned slightly to form the cutting hook. Repeat on the opposite edge. Bevelled edges are treated in the same manner, the burnisher held at the required bevel angle.

In due course burnishing alone will not be sufficient and the cutting edge will need to be reshaped. This is not difficult but it is tricky enough to require experience. The best way to learn is to have a good craftsman demonstrate the method. However, you can teach yourself by trial and error. Reshaping and sharpening a scraper blade is known as dressing the blade.

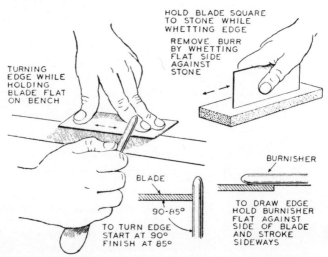

Dressing a square-edge scraper. Grind, file or whet to produce a smooth square edge. Then draw and turn to form the hook

Dressing a Hand Scraper Blade
For a scraper blade to work efficiently its cutting edge must be perfectly square and level. It should not be hollow in the centre. A worn blade is trued up first by filing or grinding, then by rubbing on an oilstone.

Dressing a Square Edge
Clamp the blade in a vice and draw-file the edge of the blade. Use a smooth file. Check to see it is level, using a try square or straight edge against the light. Round each corner very slightly so they do not dig in. Then, holding the blade square to the surface of the stone, rub on a smooth oilstone to remove the roughness left by the file. Do not allow the blade to rock from side to side or a rounded edge will result. A square edge is necessary; a rounded edge is useless. Next, lay the scraper

156

flat on the oilstone and rub to remove the burr produced by dressing the edge. The edge should be very smooth, square and fairly sharp and it is now ready for burnishing as described previously.

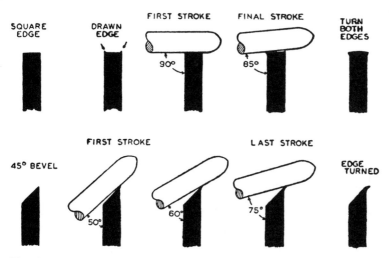

Turning a scraper blade to form the hook. Above is a square-edge scraper. The method of turning a bevel-edge scraper is shown below

Dressing a Bevel Edge
File or grind the edge to a 45° bevel. Whet the bevel side of the blade on an oilstone, holding the scraper blade as you would when sharpening a plane iron. Then, laying the face side of the blade flat on the oilstone, rub away the burr to leave a smooth edge ready for burnishing. The first few strokes with the burnisher should be at an angle which is only slightly greater than the bevel. Increase the angle with each stroke until at the final stroke the burnisher is at an angle of about 75° to the face of the blade. This produces a fast cutting edge.

Dressing a Double-handed Scraper Blade
Remove the blade from the tool and remove any remaining hook edge with a flat file held flat against the side of the blade. Then restore the old bevel by filing or grinding it to an angle

of 45°. Whet the bevel on an oilstone, maintaining the 45° bevel, until a slight burr extends along the full width of the blade. Then, with the bevel uppermost, rub the blade flat on the oilstone to remove the burr to leave a smooth, sharp edge. To burnish the blade first lay it bevel side down with its edge projecting slightly over the edge of the bench and, holding the burnisher flat against the flat side of the blade, rub it firmly back and forth along the edge. This consolidates the metal. Finally the blade is held in the vice, with the bevel edge up and the edge turned. Again the burnisher is held at an angle of 3° or 4° greater than the bevel to begin with, the angle increasing with each stroke to finish at about 75° to the face of the blade.

Abrasives

An abrasive is a hard material which wears away a softer material when both are rubbed together. Common examples are grindstones and oilstones used for sharpening tools and the coated abrasive sheets and discs used to smooth wood and other materials.

The old term 'sandpaper' is still often used, albeit incorrectly, as a general term for abrasive sheets, and sanding or sanding down to describe their use. Sand is no longer used in the manufacture of abrasive sheets, however, the modern materials being either flint or ground glass, garnet, aluminium oxide or silicone carbide. The first two have paper backing, while the last two have either paper or cloth backing. A recent introduction is tungsten carbide, the hardest-known abrasive. Grains of this material are usually bonded to a thin metal backing.

The most common and least expensive abrasive is flint or glass paper. Sand coloured, it gives satisfactory results but wears out quickly and clogs with wood dust easily. When this last happens the effectiveness of an abrasive is greatly reduced. Garnet paper, which is covered in crushed, natural red garnet, is more expensive but has better wearing qualities and gives a superior finish. Aluminium oxide, a synthetic material, is dark brown or green in colour and is tough and very hardwearing. It is most effectively used for working on hardwoods and for machine sanding. Aluminium oxide sheets can be cleaned and reused several times. Another synthetic material, silicone carbide (better known as 'wet and dry'), is black in colour. It may be used dry or with a lubricant which reduces dust and prevents clogging. It may also be used on a wide range of materials other than wood.

Coated abrasives are available in standard sheet sizes of 11in × 9in (279mm × 228mm) and also in rolls. They are obtainable in coarse, medium and fine grades but are more accurately graded within each category according to a number which relates to grit size, ie the size of the abrasive grains used. A small grit number indicates large-sized grains and therefore a coarse abrasive, a large number, small grains and a fine abrasive. In addition, the grain spacing may also be specified. Complete coverage of the backing surface is known as regular or closed coat; this cuts quickly but clogs with dust easily. Wide space grains or open coat means a surface coating of between 50 and 70 per cent; this does not clog easily but it is slower cutting.

The grading of the different types of coated abrasives is a little confusing. Some sheet material is known by a grade code, some by its grit size; in Europe, grit sizes conform to an agreed 'P' standard. American grit sizes are similar to the European coarse grades but very different from the finer grades. A comparative table is given below.

Comparative Grading Chart for Coated Abrasives

		European Products			
American Equivalents	Grit Sizes (P)	Aluminium Oxide	Silicon Carbide	Garnet Paper	Glass Paper
600	1200	—	1200	—	—
500	1000	—	1000	—	—
400	800	—	800	—	—
360	600	—	600	—	—
	500	—	500	—	—

Comparative Grading Chart for Coated Abrasives
European Products

American Equivalents	Grit Sizes (P)	Aluminium Oxide	Silicon Carbide	Garnet Paper	Glass Paper
320	400	400	400	—	—
	360	—	360	—	—
280	350	—	—	—	—
	320	320	320	9/0	—
240	280	280	280	8/0	—
	240	240	240	7/0	00 (Flour)
	220	220	220	6/0	—
	200	—	—	—	0
	180	180	180	5/0	—
	150	150	150	4/0	1
	120	120	120	3/0	$1\frac{1}{2}$
Similar to European grades	100	100	100	2/0	F2
	80	80	80	0	—
	70	—	—	—	M2
	60	60	60	$\frac{1}{2}$	—
	50	50	50	1	—
	40	40	40	$1\frac{1}{2}$	S2
	36	36	36	2	$2\frac{1}{2}$
	30	30	30	$2\frac{1}{2}$	3
	24	24	24	3	—
	20	20	20	—	—
	16	16	16	—	—

Using an Abrasive Sheet

All shaping work with chisels, planes, scrapers and other edge tools must normally be completed before abrasive materials are used. When wood is 'sanded', minute particles of grit become loosened from the paper and embedded in the wood surface. These quickly dull edge tools.

All surfaces should be sanded with the grain. Sanding across the grain tears and roughens the surface fibres and produces scratches which show through the finish. In fact, all sanding processes produce scratches. Each finer grade used makes the scratches smaller until finally they become invisible to the naked eye. That is why work should be sanded using progressively finer grades or grits. It should be remembered that, although some machine sanding processes may be used to shape work or to remove excess material, all hand sanding is intended as a finishing and not a shaping process.

For hand sanding, 11in × 9in (279mm × 228mm) sheets are best folded and torn or cut into handier sizes. One way is to divide the sheet in half, then to fold each separate piece twice to give three working surfaces. Paper-backed sheets can be torn by placing the fold over the edge of a bench or by using a steel rule as a straight edge.

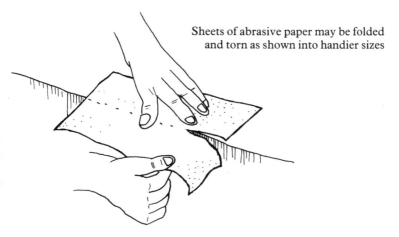

Sheets of abrasive paper may be folded and torn as shown into handier sizes

Sanding must be done carefully to avoid rounding corners and edges which are not supposed to be rounded. In many instances it is just as necessary to sand an edge squarely as it is to plane it squarely. The abrasive paper can be held in the fingers but, if it is wrapped around a rectangular block of some kind, rounding edges and some of the other pitfalls of sanding can be more easily avoided. A block of softwood approximately 5in × 3in × 1in (127mm × 176mm × 25mm) is a handy size to use. Much better than the block of wood is a block of cork of the same dimensions. A half sheet $5\frac{1}{2}$in × 9in (140mm × 228mm), obtained by tearing a full-sized sheet in half, can conveniently be wrapped around the block. It is held in place with thumb and fingers and moved round the block so that each surface of the sheet is used in turn. More even pressure can be applied when using a sanding block and a better surface produced. Concave surfaces are sanded with the paper wrapped round a piece of dowel or something

161

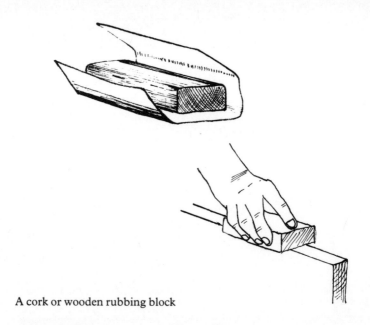

A cork or wooden rubbing block

similar. Most convex surfaces can be sanded with the paper held in the hollow of the hand.

The life of an abrasive sheet can be extended if the dust which clogs its surface is eliminated by slapping it against a hard surface once in a while.

It should not normally be necessary to begin sanding with too rough a grade of paper. Most good craftsmen prefer to reach a fairly good standard of finish with an edged tool and to give only light sanding with a fine grade paper. Flour grade or 00 flint/glass paper or 8/0 garnet paper for preference should give an adequate finish. Check work for smoothness by examining the surface at different angles to the light. Even the tiniest scratches which may hardly show will be exaggerated when the work is varnished and especially so if it is stained.

Steel wire wool is also an effective abrasive for certain applications. The finer grades are useful for finishing wood surfaces.

11
Tool Sharpening

Experienced craftsmen know the value of sharp tools. A dull tool requires a lot more driving power than a sharp one; it does its work more slowly and less accurately. A dull cutting edge makes a tool more dangerous to use than one which is sharp. The time required to sharpen dull tools is regained many times over in quality of workmanship and quicker operations.

All cutting tools become dull with use and need to be resharpened, and the proper sharpening of tools is one of the most important things to be learned. To cut accurately and easily saws need to be properly sharpened and set. To be in first-class condition, edged tools such as chisels and planes etc should not only be ground to the correct angle but they should be honed until they are sharp enough to shave a hair off the back of your hand.

Files are used to sharpen saws and auger bits. Oilstones are used to renew the cutting edges of planes, chisels and gouges etc. After the latter have been resharpened several times it may be necessary to restore the original bevel by grinding. A badly nicked edge must be ground also.

Saw Fitting

The teeth of hand saws do their cutting with their edges and points. Consequently these must be kept sharp and in good condition for the saw to cut efficiently. The complete process of saw sharpening is called fitting or refitting and involves four operations: jointing or topping, shaping, setting and filing. Filing is the actual sharpening stage.

Saw fitting is a skilled operation and requires experience and patience. If you can file accurately, you can sharpen a saw after some practice. Efficient saw fitting demands a steady hand and good eyesight and the filing stroke must be kept level at all times. If you cannot file properly or if a saw is badly worn or damaged, it is best refitted by a skilled saw doctor.

The teeth of most saws are slightly bent or are 'set' alternately to the left and right along the blade so that the slot cut in the work, the 'kerf', is wider than the thickness of the saw blade. By thus reducing the friction between the blade and the work, it makes sawing easier. Teeth usually need resetting if a saw has been used considerably before being resharpened. However, it is not necessary to reset the teeth every time a saw is filed sharp. In most instances a saw may be sharpened four or five times before it needs resetting. A hand saw is best treated like a knife or chisel and touched up every once in a while to keep its edge keen. The saw will then cut longer and better, its set will remain effective and the angles of the teeth will be easier to follow in subsequent refitting.

The 'set' on the cutting teeth of a saw

Recognising a Dull Saw

A good craftsman can tell when a saw is dull or when it needs resetting, by its feel when he cuts wood with it. A saw which has to be forced into the wood probably needs sharpening. If it continually jams in the kerf or wanders from the cutting line it needs resetting. He can also tell by examining the teeth closely. If the teeth are uneven, if the points and edges are not sharp or if there is not enough set he can see it. Edges and points are easier to see when they are dull. Sharp edges and points are almost invisible.

Study the teeth of a new saw or one resharpened by an expert. Then look and feel the edge of a saw which has had a great deal of use. The difference is readily obvious.

Necessary Equipment

To refit a saw properly, the blade must be held rigidly in a vice or special clamp. The best equipment for this purpose is a saw vice or a portable wooden saw horse. The best substitute is a large bench vice and two straight pieces of hardwood about $12\text{in} \times 2\text{in} \times \frac{3}{4}\text{in}$ ($305\text{mm} \times 50\text{mm} \times 19\text{mm}$). The saw blade is put between the wood strips and clamped in the vice. The strips should be parallel to the toothed edge which should not project too far above them. The saw must be held firmly so that it does not vibrate when filed. The teeth directly above the vice jaws are held most firmly. File at this point and move the saw blade along as the work proceeds. Work where there is plenty of light so that the teeth can be plainly seen.

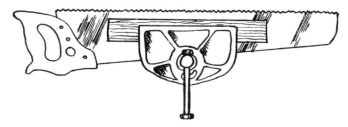

Refitting a saw—the saw must be firmly held

Topping or jointing is done with an 8in (203mm) or 10in (254mm) smooth, flat mill file or with a special jointing tool. The latter hinges open and is clamped over the toothed edge of the blade and run back and forth along the teeth. If a file is used it can be held in an easily made hardwood block. Both the jointing tool and the wood block eliminate any chance of tipping the file so that the points of the teeth become rounded at the sides.

For shaping and for sharpening, the files used are triangular in section. They must be of the correct type, cut and size for the kind of saw and the kind of teeth to be filed. They are single-cut files, are made in various sizes and are called slim taper files.

Generally speaking a file with faces twice as wide as the

165

depth of the gullet (the 'V'-shaped space between the teeth) is suitable. The exact size of file to use is determined by the saw's number of tooth points per inch.

For setting saw teeth the easiest tool to use is the pliers-type sawset. This is adjustable to the required set of the saw and when placed over alternate teeth gives the correct angle and depth of set each time the sawset handle is squeezed.

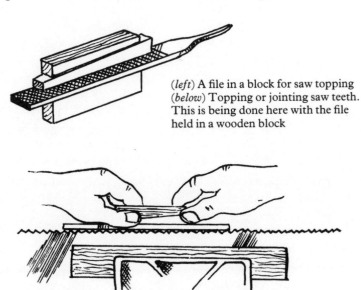

(*left*) A file in a block for saw topping (*below*) Topping or jointing saw teeth. This is being done here with the file held in a wooden block

Topping or Jointing

The teeth of a saw must all be brought to the same height before any other stage can be carried out successfully. This is done by passing the jointer or file lightly back and forth along the blade. A flat area of bright metal will show when each tooth has been touched. Stop when all the teeth show this mark. Do not overfile or much more reshaping will be necessary at the next stage. If some teeth appear overfiled while some are not touched, it will be necessary to carry out some shaping at this stage and to top the saw again, otherwise the correct tooth spacing may be lost.

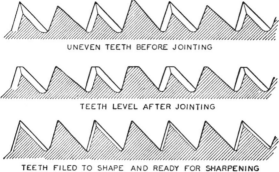

UNEVEN TEETH BEFORE JOINTING

TEETH LEVEL AFTER JOINTING

TEETH FILED TO SHAPE AND READY FOR SHARPENING

Jointing saw teeth evens them prior to setting and filing. It is not necessary unless the points of the teeth are uneven

Shaping

The teeth may now need restoring to their original size and shape by further filing, this time in the gullets between the teeth points. If the saw has been only lightly topped, this stage may be omitted as a separate operation and combined with sharpening. A triangular file is used, one the same size as recommended for sharpening that particular saw. The object here is to retain the required depth and 'pitch' of each tooth, pitch being the angle at which the teeth lean towards the front

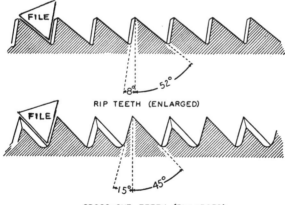

RIP TEETH (ENLARGED)

CROSS-CUT TEETH (ENLARGED)

Rip and cross-cut teeth. The rip saw tooth has an angle of 8° on the front and 52° on the back. The front of the cross-cut saw tooth should have an angle of 15° and the back of the tooth an angle of 45°

167

or toe of the saw. Pitch varies according to the type of saw as shown by the diagram.

The saw is held, handle to the right and shaping begun at the heel of the saw, ie nearest the handle. Teeth at this end will be almost unused and therefore of the original shape and pitch. Let these be your guide and allow the file to bear against the edges it touches.

Hold the file handle in one hand, finger tips of the other holding the end of the file. Keep the file at right angles to the blade and file straight across. Use a controlled, light, forward cutting stroke and lift the file clear on the back stroke. File each gullet in turn until the teeth are uniform in size and shape, removing the flat area made when topping the saw. A burr will have been formed and this is removed by rubbing an oilstone lightly along the side of the blade. This is known as side dressing the saw.

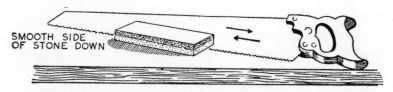

SMOOTH SIDE OF STONE DOWN

Dressing the teeth. After filing and before setting, lay the saw flat on a bench or table and rub a fine oilstone lightly over the teeth to remove any burr or wire edge. Dress both sides of the saw in this way

Setting

After shaping it will be necessary to reset the teeth, that is to offset alternate teeth to left and right as described. Adjust the sawset to suit the saw. This ensures that each tooth is given the correct and the same amount of set and depth of set. All the teeth must project by the same amount on each side, otherwise the saw will pull to one side, run out of line and fail to cut true. The depth of set should be no more than half the depth of the tooth; too much set and the teeth are liable to crack and break off. Always set teeth in the same direction in which they were previously set.

168

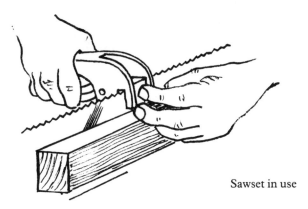

Sawset in use

In use the sawset is placed over a tooth and the plunger of the tool lined up centrally and squarely with the point of the tooth. When the handle is squeezed, the plunger presses the tooth against the anvil of the tool to give the required set. Each alternate tooth is dealt with, working from one side of the saw; the saw is then reversed in the vice or clamp and the remaining teeth set in the same way but from the opposite side.

Sharpening

As previously described in Chapter 2 the teeth of rip saws and cross-cut saws are not the same because they cut in a different way. So far the operations described for refitting saws apply to both types of saw. When sharpening, however, their treatment differs.

For sharpening, place the saw in the vice or clamp with the handle to the right and the bottom of the gullets about $\frac{1}{8}$in (3mm) above the vice jaws. If the blade is any higher, it will vibrate and chatter when filed. A chattering saw cannot be properly sharpened. Sharpening is normally begun at the toe and progresses towards the heel of the saw, the blade being moved along to the left so that the filing is always taking place above the vice jaws.

The teeth of a ripsaw are sharpened so that the tooth points are like chisel edges. Therefore they are filed level and straight across the saw with the file held at 90° to the blade. Remember to maintain the pitch angle of the teeth.

Select the first tooth that is set towards you. Place the file in the gullet to the left of that tooth. The file must sit well down in the gullet and touch evenly on two teeth—it works on the front edge of the first tooth towards you and on the back edge of the tooth to the left simultaneously. The file should cut on the push stroke only. Keep the file level and at right angles to the blade at all times. File every alternative gullet, always to the left of a tooth set towards you.

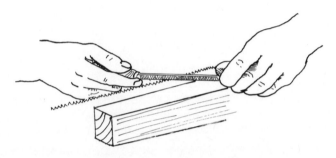

Sharpening with a triangular file

When one side is completed, reverse the saw in the vice so that the handle is to the left. Starting again at the toe, begin filing in the first gullet missed out when filing from the opposite side. File every other gullet as before all the way to the handle.

If the teeth have been properly reshaped and are uniform in size, it is best to give each tooth the same number of strokes with the file so as to maintain the uniformity. When the saw has only been lightly topped and the reshaping stage omitted, then alternate teeth are filed until half the flat top is removed. When the saw is reversed the remaining half is filed away and the point of each tooth brought to a sharp, square cutting edge.

Cross-cut saws are sharpened in a similar way but, in order to give the teeth their knife-like cutting edge, they are filed to a bevel so that they are pointed like the end of a knife blade. To make this bevel the file is held at an angle of about 60° to the blade of the saw. In addition the file handle is lowered slightly so that the file cuts at between 5° and 10° to the horizontal. Remember also the pitch of the teeth. It sounds complicated, but in practice it becomes more easy to understand.

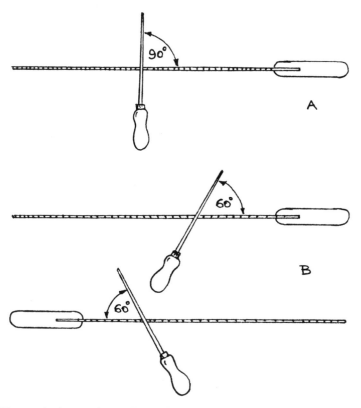

Filing angles in saw sharpening. A for a rip saw, 90°; B for a cross–cut saw, 60° in alternate directions

If the teeth are of the correct shape to begin with, then the file should rest firmly in the gullet at the proper pitch angle. With the saw held as described, position the file in the gullet to the left of the first tooth set towards you and tilt the handle down slightly. Then bring the handle of the file over to the

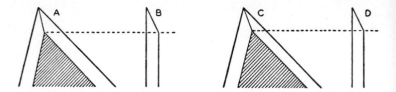

The bevel is important. Too much bevel causes the point of the teeth to score too deeply and the kerf to clog. Teeth bevelled to a long front as at A and B are best suited to softwoods. A shorter bevel as shown at C and D is best for medium-hardwoods

left, away from the handle of the saw so that the file is at an angle of about 60° to the saw blade. Lines marked on the bench or vice clamp at the required angle will help keep the bevel constant.

Let the file cut only on the forward stroke as before and remember that you are filing the back of the tooth to the left and the front of the tooth to the right simultaneously. Slightly more pressure on the back edge than on the front edge will make the filing easier and more effective. After sharpening, a light side dressing with an oilstone may be given to true up the set and cut of the saw.

Tenon saws, dovetail saws, etc, cut in the same way as the cross-cut and so are sharpened in the same way. Because of their many, small teeth greater care is needed in refitting. Such saws ought only to be attempted by skilled workmen, especially if the saw is very worn.

Sharpening a Log Saw
The common type of cross-cut or jack saw used for hand sawing of logs and large timbers uses replaceable blades. These can be sharpened with a file to prolong their useful life. They have two different kinds of teeth known as cutters and rakers. The cutters cut while the rakers give clearance in the cut so that the blade does not jam in wet wood. When new the raker teeth are slightly below the cutting edge of the cutters.

First top or joint the teeth as described, then a smooth mill file is used to file all the cutting teeth to a sharp point. A bevel must be produced and this is achieved by holding the file at an angle of about 45° to the blade. This gives a fast cutting edge.

The raker teeth are filed at 90° or straight across the blade to bring them just below the cutters. If the blade has been sharpened several times, it may be necessary to deepen the gullets between the teeth. This is done with a round edged file.

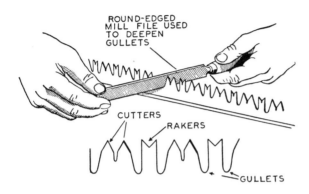

Sharpening a large cross-cut saw. The teeth should be sharpened by filing with a mill file or a special cross-cut file. A round-edged mill file is used to deepen the gullets when necessary

Sharpening an Edge-cutting Tool

This section includes chisels, gouges, plane blades and knives. All of these are sharpened on an oilstone. Some may require reshaping on a revolving grindstone before sharpening.

Oilstones

There are two types: natural and artificial. The best are the natural stones cut from rock quarried in Arkansas in the USA. These come in various grades: Soft, Hard and Black Hard Arkansas and Washita. Oilstones made from a certain Welsh slate are used by some craftsmen. Artificial stones appear under the names India, Carborundum and Crystolon etc, and are available in fine, medium and coarse grades. To sharpen tools properly it is necessary to have a coarse or hard stone for fast cutting and a fine or soft stone for putting on a

173

finished edge. Natural stones normally give the best finished edge. Combination stones giving a fast cutting surface on one side and a slower cutting surface on the other are available.

Sharpening stones are called oilstones because when in use they are kept wct with oil. The pores of a dry stone become clogged with fine particles of steel rubbed from blades being sharpened. A clogged stone loses much of its cutting ability. The oil floats off the fine particles and prevents the stone becoming clogged. It also lubricates the tool being sharpened, preventing friction and overheating.

The oil used must be thin and must not gum. Thick vegetable oils clog the pores of the stone. A mixture of equal parts of light machine oil and paraffin (kerosene) works well on most stones.

Oilstones for bench use are usually available in two sizes: 6in × 2in × 1in (152mm × 50mm × 25mm) and 8in × 2in × 1in (204mm × 50mm × 25mm). They should be kept in a substantial wooden box made for the purpose and kept covered with a lid when not in use. This prevents the stone getting damaged—they are quite brittle and are easily chipped or broken. The lid keeps workshop dust off the surface. Various, small, shaped stones called slipstones are also available. These are made mainly for sharpening shaped gouges etc.

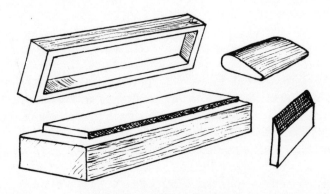

A boxed oilstone and two slipstones

When a stone becomes clogged up or gummy, it will have a black glazed surface. It can be cleaned and reconditioned by being soaked overnight in paraffin and then scrubbed with clean paraffin and a stiff brush. Alternatively it may be heated in a warm oven until the oil and dirt oozes from the surface and wiped clean whilst it is still warm. Do not get it too hot or the stone will crack.

In use an oilstone should have its entire surface used. Some advocate a figure-of-eight motion of the chisel blade when honing. Do not consistently rub narrow chisels up and down the centre of the stone. This causes the stone surface to become hollow and it becomes increasingly difficult to bring larger chisels and especially plane irons to a true, straight edge. The stone needs dressing if it becomes hollow.

A flat, smooth surface is necessary—an iron plate or a sheet of glass or plastic laminate is suitable. For natural stones you will need a small handful of silver sand, and for artificial stones about half an ounce (15gr) of aluminium oxide powder of a grit size slightly coarser than that of the stone to be dressed. Mix either of these with a little water to resemble thin mud. Smear this all over the flat surface and lay the worn oilstone on it face down. Using both hands bear down with moderate pressure and scrub the stone around with a circular motion. Examine the surface of the oilstone from time to time and it will be seen that the hollow is disappearing and the stone will in due course become perfectly flat. Wipe clean and re-oil and the stone is as good as new again.

Sharpening a Chisel

Accurate work cannot be done with a dull chisel. This is especially true when cutting across the grain of hardwood. A dull tool is difficult and dangerous to use. More cut hands result from pressing too hard with a chisel which is not sharp than from working with one which has a really keen cutting edge.

Chisels are ground on a grindstone in order to restore the

angle of the bevel. It is not necessary to regrind the bevel each time the cutting edge becomes dull. Normal sharpening is carried out using a coarse or medium oilstone and a smooth stone for the finished edge. This work is usually referred to as honing or whetting.

One of the important things to know about a chisel is that it has two bevels. Normally the large bevel is at an angle of 25 to 30°. This is put on by grinding on a grindstone. The second or smaller bevel is known as the honing or whetting bevel—sometimes the sharpening angle. This is usually at 30 to 35° and is made on the oilstone. To obtain this sharpening angle the chisel is held to the oilstone so that the whole of the large bevel is in contact with its surface. Then by raising the chisel handle slightly the back edge of the ground bevel comes off the stone so that its front edge can be honed sharp.

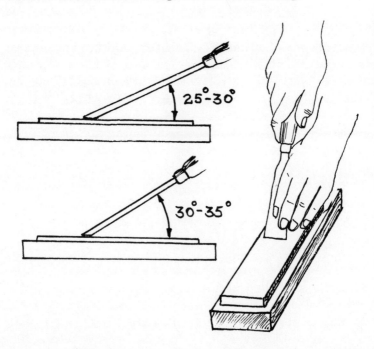

Sharpening a chisel. Note the two angles—the first is the grinding angle, the second the sharpening angle

176

The oilstone should be held at bench level so that it cannot slide about. A boxed stone may be gripped in the vice. Grip the chisel handle in the right hand and use the first and second fingers of the left low down on the blade to hold it firmly against the face of the stone. With moderate pressure only rub the chisel back and forth on the stone with smooth, even strokes. Apply slightly more pressure on the forward stroke. The sharpening action will produce a burr or wire edge on the top of the blade and sharpening should continue until this extends all the way across the cutting edge.

Keep the hands steady and the wrists stiff whilst doing this. Do not rock the blade or the bevel will be rounded and will not cut properly. And keep the chisel square with the sides of the stone, otherwise the cutting edge will become skewed and difficult to control.

For sharpening chisels and plane irons there is a very convenient gadget known as a honing guide. This removes a large part of the guesswork and gives the beginner a better chance.

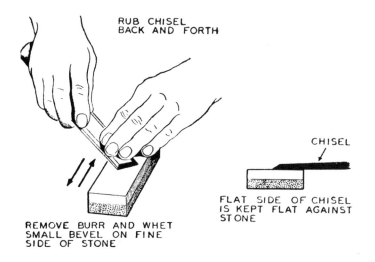

RUB CHISEL BACK AND FORTH

CHISEL

FLAT SIDE OF CHISEL IS KEPT FLAT AGAINST STONE

REMOVE BURR AND WHET SMALL BEVEL ON FINE SIDE OF STONE

Removing the burr—a feather edge raised on the back of the chisel during sharpening

177

Removing the Burr

The burr, wire edge or feather edge—it is known by all three names—is not wanted and is removed by a few strokes with the flat side of the chisel blade held absolutely flat on a fine stone. Be careful not to raise the blade even slightly whilst honing the back of the chisel. Next, still using the fine stone, take several light strokes with the chisel held bevel down and finish with two or three more strokes flat side down again. This should remove the burr completely to leave a fine, keen cutting edge.

Many give a finishing touch to the edge by stropping it a few times on a leather or canvas strop. This is oil soaked or it may be dressed with a mild abrasive such as crocus powder or jeweller's rouge.

Testing the Edge

Many craftsmen judge the sharpness of an edge by testing it on a thumbnail or by carefully feeling it with the ball of the thumb. Your eye should tell you whether you have produced a really sharp edge by honing. Hold the chisel where a good light will shine on the cutting edge. A keen edge does not reflect light. If you see a white line or any patches of reflected light it is not a sharp edge.

Sharpening a Gouge

Sharpening a gouge is much the same as sharpening a chisel. As already explained in Chapter 4 there are gouges with their bevel ground on the inside and those with it ground on the outside.

An outside bevel gouge can be sharpened on a flat oilstone, the gouge held at right angles to the stone and the blade moved across its surface with a rolling movement. A special wedge-shaped, grooved stone is available. The gouge is stroked back and forth in the most suitable part of the groove. Most often shaped slipstones are used.

For inside bevel gouges shaped slipstones are essential; different sizes and radii are required to suit the gouges to be

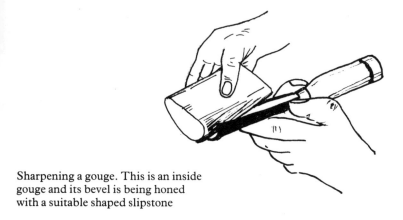

Sharpening a gouge. This is an inside
gouge and its bevel is being honed
with a suitable shaped slipstone

sharpened. When honing these concave bevels, instead of
moving the tool over the stone, hold it still and rub with the
stone. A slight rotary motion should be given. When
removing any burr take care not to produce even the slightest
bevel on the flat side of the gouge.

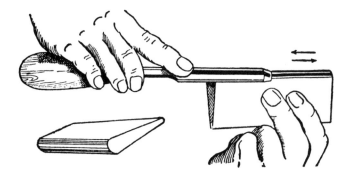

Removing the burr. This is an outside gouge and the burr raised when
sharpening is being removed with a fine slipstone

Sharpening a Plane Iron

Sharpening a plane iron or blade is like sharpening a chisel.
Like the chisel, the plane iron has two bevels, a grinding bevel
and a honing bevel. Ordinarily the edge may be honed on an
oilstone several times before its bevel needs regrinding.

The first thing to do after removing the iron from the plane
is to separate the cutting iron from the cap iron (if it is a

179

double iron plane). This is done by loosening the cap screw and sliding it along to the end of the slot where the screw head will pass through the hole. A plane cutting iron cannot be sharpened with the cap iron in place.

The honing process is begun by holding the plane iron bevel-side down to the surface of an oilstone. Hold the iron in the right hand, two fingers of the left down near the cutting edge to hold it firmly to the surface of the stone. At first the whole bevel should be in contact with the stone. Then the back edge is raised very slightly to give the correct sharpening angle. For general use the grinding angle is 25 to 30°, the honing or sharpening angle, 30 to 35°.

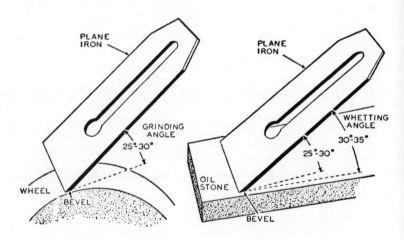

The correct grinding and whetting angles for plane irons

Hold the iron firmly, keep an even, moderate pressure against the stone and, with the wrists stiff, move the hands parallel to the stone. Make sure that all parts of the cutting edge come into contact with the stone as it is stroked back and forth. The main pressure should be on the forward stroke, and the angle between the iron and the stone must be kept constant. Again raise a burr all along the cutting edge; usually six to a dozen strokes will be enough.

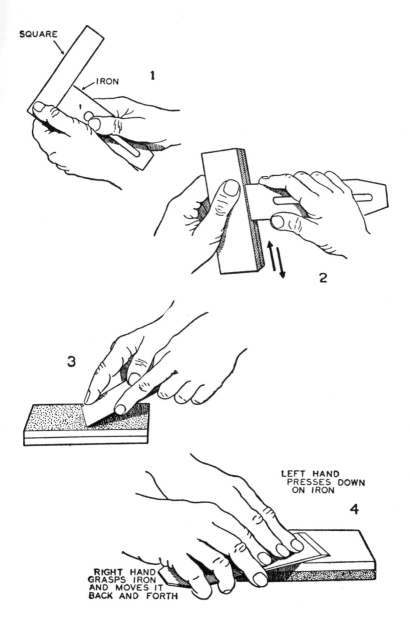

Whetting a plane iron. 1 Testing the edge of a plane iron for squareness. 2 Squaring an edge by rubbing it against the side of an oilstone. 3 Whetting the bevel side. 4 Whetting the flat side to remove a wire edge

181

The plane iron is then turned over and its flat side rubbed back and forth a few times to remove the burr. Keep both hands on the iron to avoid any possibility of lifting it. It must be kept *absolutely* flat.

If the burr is not removed after a few strokes with the flat side of the blade held flat on the stone, hone with the bevel side down again for a few strokes. Usually the burr will break away to leave a good cutting edge. Check for sharpness as described for chisels. Use a strop to finish off if one is available. Wipe clean on completion.

To avoid plane marks on wide surfaces, plane irons for smoothing planes are sharpened with a straight cutting edge but with slightly rounded corners. Jack plane blades are given a slight curvature across their width for faster cutting.

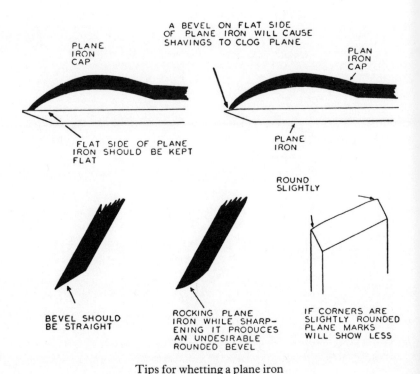

Tips for whetting a plane iron

Assembling a Double Iron

A newly sharpened plane iron must be handled carefully to avoid nicking its keen edge. A nicked cutting edge leaves a raised score mark across the surface being planed. To assemble a double iron, lay the plane iron across the flat side of the plane iron with the screw in the hole in the slot. Then pull it down and away from the cutting edge and when it is almost at the bottom of the slot turn the cap parallel to the

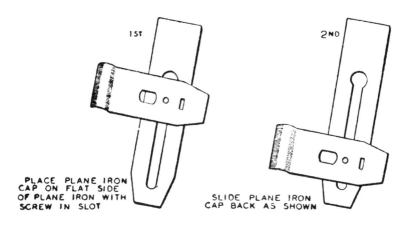

1ST

PLACE PLANE IRON CAP ON FLAT SIDE OF PLANE IRON WITH SCREW IN SLOT

2ND

SLIDE PLANE IRON CAP BACK AS SHOWN

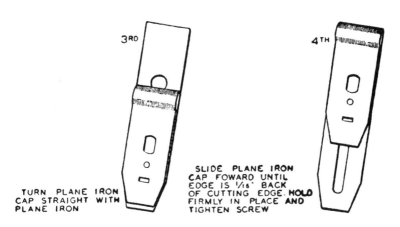

3RD

TURN PLANE IRON CAP STRAIGHT WITH PLANE IRON

4TH

SLIDE PLANE IRON CAP FOWARD UNTIL EDGE IS 1/16" BACK OF CUTTING EDGE. HOLD FIRMLY IN PLACE AND TIGHTEN SCREW

How to assemble a double plane iron

cutter. Holding both together slide the cap forward towards the cutting edge. The cap should never be moved across the cutting edge. For general work the edge of the cap iron should be about $\frac{1}{16}$in (1·5mm) back from the cutting edge (see Chapter 3). When in position hold cap and iron firmly together and tighten the screw which holds them together.

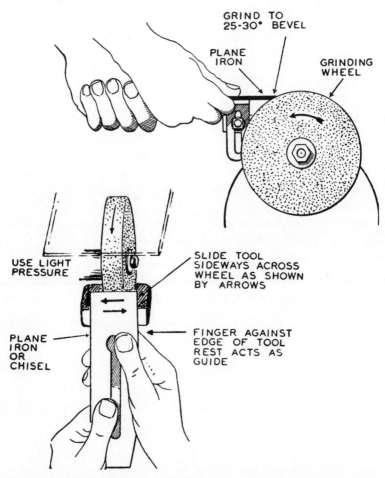

Grinding a plane iron or chisel. Both hands are needed to hold the tool. Dip the tool in water frequently to cool the edge and keep it from burning. The lower sketch shows the position of the tool and of the hands (looking down on them)

Grinding

The amateur craftsman who uses his tools only occasionally will seldom need to grind them. They can be kept sharp by honing as described. However, in time, bevels become worn or cutting edges may be accidentally damaged and then they must be reground.

A variety of revolving grinding wheels may be used; the best are kept wet with water or oil but the engineer's bench grinder is often used. Grinding attachments for power drills are also available (see Chapter 9). These have dry carborundum wheels and their use requires care and experience. The hazard of using dry, high speed wheels is the risk of seriously overheating the steel. This takes the temper from the blade and softens it. Soft steel will not keep a good cutting edge. When a blade is overheated it turns blue in colour. With care this can be avoided—dipping the blade in water frequently will help keep it cool. It is not as easy as it looks.

Grinders should be adequately guarded and the user should wear goggles to protect his eyes. It should have a close fitting tool rest and preferably one which can be adjusted to the required grinding angle.

Sharpening a Boring Tool

When twist drills and auger bits etc. become dull through constant use or have their cutting edges bruised by encounters with hidden nails or screws, then they must be resharpened. If not, not only will drilling by hand be strenuous but also holes bored will not be accurate as the drill will wander off course. Blunt drills used in a power drill will overheat through friction. Drilling hardwood will blunt drills quicker than drilling softwood.

Sharpening an Auger Bit
An auger bit can be resharpened by filing, ideally using a special auger-bit file. This file is small, double-ended and tapered so that the narrow portion can be used on small

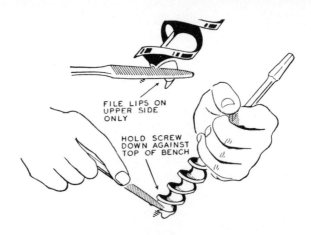

FILE LIPS ON UPPER SIDE ONLY

HOLD SCREW DOWN AGAINST TOP OF BENCH

Filing the lips of an auger bit

diameter bits and the wider portion on larger bits. One end of the file is made with its sides 'safe' or smooth, while the other has cut edges. In sharpening an auger bit both the lips and the spurs or nibs are filed. The safe portion of the special file makes it easier to file both without damaging adjacent surfaces. Small, smooth, flat or triangular files can be used to give an extra keen edge. Do not oversharpen; there is very little metal to spare and too much filing unnecessarily reduces the life of the bit.

When being sharpened the bit may be held upright in a vice

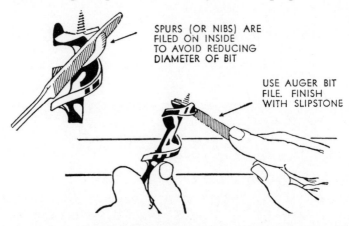

SPURS (OR NIBS) ARE FILED ON INSIDE TO AVOID REDUCING DIAMETER OF BIT

USE AUGER BIT FILE. FINISH WITH SLIPSTONE

Filing the nibs of an auger bit

186

or firmly held down against the top of the bench. The lips should be filed on the upper surface of the cutting edge only, ie the edge towards the shank. Follow the original bevel and file an equal amount from each lip. The spurs are filed on the *inside* only in order to maintain the diameter of the bit. Spurs should be filed across their entire inside surface rather than just the leading edge.

Centre bits are sharpened in the same way as described for auger bits. The centre point of the old type centre bit can be touched up with a file but the centre screw on auger and improved centre bits should never be filed.

Sharpening a Forstner Bit
Only the cutting lips or nibs are sharpened on this type of bit. A thin, flat file (or an auger-bit file) which will fit through the throat of the bit is needed. File as described for sharpening the cutting lips of the auger bit. Do not attempt to sharpen the rim. The saw-toothed bit is sharpened in the same way. In addition the top edges of the teeth may also be lightly touched with a smooth file or slip stone; take care to maintain the same bevels to give clearance.

Sharpening a Flat Bit
Lightly file the forward cutting edges, maintaining the original bevel and keeping the filed surface flat and even. If the brad point is sharpened, take care to keep its point central, otherwise it will cause the drill to pull to one side in use.

Sharpening a Twist Drill
This drill is normally sharpened on a revolving, fine-grit grindstone. The drill is held to the stone at the required angle (45° for wood and about 60° for metal) and the cutting edge rotated slowly anticlockwise. Lift the drill at the same time as it is rotated. Repeat for the other cutting edge. Keep the centre of the drill central and do not attempt to grind it to a sharp point.

Index

Abrasives, 158–62; grading chart, 159–60; types, 158; use of, 160–2
Adhesives, 111–22; animal, 113, 118; casein, 113, 117; PVA, 111, 116; synthetic resin, 111, 116
Aluminium oxide paper, 159
Auger bits, 125–7; to sharpen, 185–7

Back saws, 30–3
Bench stop (or hook), 41
Bevel-edge chisel, 61
Bits, 125–30; auger, 125; centre, 127; countersink, 129; dowel, 127; expansive, 128; flat, 129; Forstner, 127, 187; saw tooth, 128; screwdriver, 100; to sharpen, 185–7; twist, 130; *see also* Drills
Blades: plane, 40; screwdriver, 98, 100
Block plane, 50
Boring, *see* Drilling
Bow saw, 39
Brace, 123
Brass screws, to prevent twisting off, 106
Bull nose plane, 52–3
Burnisher, 155
Burnishing, 155, 157, 158

Cabinet: rasps, 75; scrapers, 151; screwdriver, 98
Carving tools, 73
Chamfering, with a chisel, 68
Chiselling, 63–72
Chisels: bevel-edge, 61; butt, 62; firmer, 61; mortice, 62; paring, 61; to sharpen, 175–8; socket, 61; tang, 59; types, 61–2
Claw hammer, 77
Clinching (or clenching) nails, 84
Compass saw, 35
Coping saw, 37
Cramping, 116; *see also* Gluing
Cramps (or clamps), 115, 117, 119
Cross-cut saw: to sharpen, 166–9; use of, 26

Cross peen hammer, 79

Dividers, 20
Dovetail saws, 33
Dowel bits, 127; to glue, 122; joints, 148
Drilling (or boring): at an angle, 134; with a brace, 131; with a hand drill, 134; for screws, 104
Drills, 123–36; attachments for, electric, 140–6; bits, 125–30; brace, 123, 131; breast, 125; electric, 137–40; hand, 124, 134; twist, 130
Driving screws, 102

Electric drills, 137–40; attachments, 140–8; chuck capacity, 138; drilling, 139–40; power rating, 137; speed, 138–9
End grain, to plane, 43, 50
Expansive bit, 128

Files and rasps, 74; for sharpening saws, 165
Filing saw teeth, 163–9
Finishing, *see* Sanding
Firmer chisel, 61
Folding rule, 11, 12
Forstner bits, 127, 187
Fret saw, 37

Garnet paper, 158
Gauge number, of screws, 94
Gauges: marking, 18; mortice, 19
Gauging, 17
Glasspaper, 158
Glues, *see* Adhesives
Gluing, 114–22; boards edge to edge, 118; cramping or clamping, 115; dowel joints, 122; irregular shapes, 120; mitres, 121; panels, 120
Gouges, 72–3
Grain, of wood, 23, 43
Grinding, 184–5

189

Hammers: claw, 77; cross peen (pein), 79; handles, to fit, 80-1; head, 79; ripping, 77; sizes and weights, 77-9; types, 78; use of, 81-7
Hand drill, 124
Hand saws, 23-4
Hand (or cabinet) scraper, 153
Hanger bolts, 97
Holding power, of nails, 88
Horizontal chiselling, 64-5

Iron, plane, 40, 47; to sharpen, 179

Jack plane, 44
Jointer plane, 44
Jointing (or topping) of saws, 166
Jointing, with power tools, 147-8
Joints: comb, 147; dowel, 148; mortice and tenon, 147-8

Kerf, when sawing, 23, 26, 27
Keyhole saw, 35
Knife, marking, 15, 21

Lag screws, 97
Laying out, marking out, 11-21

Mallets, 75-6
Marking: gauge, 18-19; knife, 15, 21; out, 11-21
Mitre box, 31
Mitres, to glue, 121
Mortice chisel, 62
Mortice gauge, 19

Nail hammers, *see* Hammers, claw
Nailing, 83-7; clenching (or clinching), 84; concealing, 85; drawing, 86-7; driving, 81; skew, 84; toe, 84
Nails: holding power of, 88; common, 89; copper, 91; corrugated (or wiggle), 91; cut, 90; escutcheon pins, 90; panel pins, 89; penny system, 89; roofing, 91; screw, 92; sprig, 90; staples, 92; upholstery, 90
Nail set, 85
Nail sizes, 88-92

Oilstones, 173-5; to recondition, 175; types, 173
Oilstoning: chisels, 176-8; gouges, 178; plane blades, 179-82; saw teeth, 168; scrapers, 157, 158
Old Woman's Tooth, 54

Orbital sander, 144

Panels, to glue, 120
Paring, 64
Paring chisel, 61
Pencils, 21
Penny system, 89
Philips screws and screwdrivers, 95, 99
Pilot holes, for screws, 104-5
Planes, 40-58; to adjust, 47-9; block, 50-1; circular (or compass), 57; combination, 56; fore, 44; jack, 44-5; jointer, 44; plough, 54-5; rebate (or rabbet), 51-3; router, 54; to sharpen, 179-83; shoulder, 53; smoothing, 40, 46
Planing: end grain, 43, 50; grain direction, 43; holding work, 41; with jack plane, 44; rebating, 53; with smoothing plane, 46, 47
Power tools, 137-50; attachments, 140-6; circular saw, 144; disc sander, 142-3; drum sander, 143; electric drills, 137-40; jointing with, 147-8; orbital sander, 144; sabre saw, 145-6; safety, 149-50; sawing, 144-7; single function, 149; wood turning with, 148

Rasps, 74
Rebate (or rabbet) planes, 51; use of, 52
Reconditioning oilstones, 175
Rip saw, 23, 24; to sharpen, 169-70; use of, 28
Ripping bar, 87
Ripping hammer, 77
Router, 54
Rules (or rulers), 11, 12

Sanding (or sanding down), 158, 160-2; with power tools, 141-5
Sandpaper, *see* Glasspaper
Saw files, 165
Saw fitting, 163-72
Sawing, 26, 28-9; with a back saw, 33; coping saw, 37; cross-cut saw, 26; fret saw, 37; hints for, 28-30; with power tool attachments, 144-7; rip saw, 28
Saws, 22-5, 30-9; back, 30-3; bow, 39; care of, 25; compass, 35; coping, 37; cross-cut, 26; difference between cross-cut and rip, 23-4; dovetail, 33; fret, 37; keyhole, 35; rip, 28; tenon, 31
Saw set, pliers type, 166
Saw setting, 168-9

Saw teeth (or points), 23–5
Saw vice (or saw horse), 165
Scrapers, 151–9; to sharpen, 155–8
Screwdriver bits, 100
Screwdrivers, 98–102; to dress blade of, 108–9; misuse of, 108; types and sizes, 98–101
Screws, see Wood screws
Sharpening, see Tool sharpening
Skewnailing, 84
Sliding T bevel, 16
Slipstones, 174
Smoothing and finishing, 151–62
Smoothing planes, 40–6
Socket chisel, 61
Spokeshave, 57
Squares: carpenter's, 13–14; marking out with, 15; try, 14
Squaring, across and around a board, 15–16
Surform tools, 58
Steel tape, 11

Tang chisels, 59
Toenailing, 84
Tool sharpening, 163–87; auger bits, 185–7; centre bits, 187; chisels, 175–8; flat bits, 187; Forstner bits, 187; gouges, 178; grinding, 183; plane irons, 179–83; saws, 163–73
Try squares, 14
Twist drills, 130

Vertical chiselling, 66–8
Vices: bench, 41; saw, 165

Wiggle nails, 91
Woodcarving, 73–4
Wood screws: to conceal, 106; to drive, 102; holes for, 104; Philips, 95; to remove tight, 103; sizes of, 93–5; types, 93–7
Wood turning, 148